WE HAVE A FUTURE

London: Humphrey Milford,
Oxford University Press

WE HAVE A FUTURE

NORMAN THOMAS

PRINCETON · 1941
PRINCETON UNIVERSITY PRESS

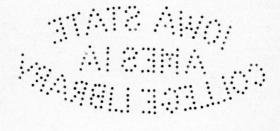

PRINTED IN THE UNITED STATES OF AMERICA
55

To
F. V. T.

PREFACE

THIS book has its origin in a desire to write simply and briefly about our country as it might be in contrast to what I fear it may become. It is a personal treatment of the questions involved, as seen against the background of more than twenty years of hard political work, including four Presidential campaigns and many other trips which have taken me into all parts of the country.

The "perpendicular pronoun" frequently occurs; yet I have tried to use it to emphasize a personal quest for the path we should take to the future rather than any oracular judgments based on infallible authority. My great preoccupation when the book was first conceived was the economic situation rather than the war. Of course the two are tied together. The war is in part an expression of a social revolution, an ugly revolution, and in part an acceleration of that revolution. So fast is the march of events that in the interval between the writing of this book and its publication the war situation may have turned sharply.

But I can imagine no events which will change my own judgment on the war, and our duty toward it. Great as may be the differences among British victory, German victory, and stalemate, the underlying forces of social change will drive us on. America's future will still be determined by the handling of internal forces rather than by the might of the most diabolical of foreign dictators. And no British victory of itself will guarantee a solution of the problems of our relation to the world, or of that sort of world organization upon which enduring peace and prosperity will depend.

Our future is still ours to shape, less absolutely than our fathers believed, but more truly than in our sudden awareness of the perils which surround us we have assumed. In thinking about that future, I have necessarily dealt with many subjects with a brevity inviting the charge of superficiality. I plead only that my intention has been to indicate the choices before us, and to present rationally the possible shapes that our future may have. Detailed blueprints must follow the great choice we make.

I am indebted to the *Saturday Evening Post* and W. W. Norton and Company for courteous permission to quote copyrighted material.

NORMAN THOMAS

CONTENTS

WE HAVE A FUTURE

CHAPTER I ☆ THE LOST WORLD OF OUR YOUTH

W E WHOSE youth fell before the First World War have already lived through a change in the social order as definite and inexorable as any of the great revolutions in history. For us Americans, although not for our European brethren, that change as yet has been less dramatic than the withdrawal of the Roman Legions from Britain, or the years following the fall of the Bastille in France, or the passing of the old order in the South with the defeat of the Confederacy. It has been equally significant and more universal.

No wishful thinking, no grim determination, no military victory can restore the world that is gone.

To thoughtful men and women in Europe it would be underscoring the obvious to insist on this point, but in our own country, 1940 saw millions of men marshalled in an election campaign to restore the economic order of William McKinley, mysteriously reconciled with the reforms of Franklin Roosevelt.

Powerful sections of the upper and middle classes have turned to armament economics, imperialism, and even war to save their order, almost as instinctively as the moth turns to the flame—and as fatally. There are choices, and desirable choices, which we in America can still make effective. They do not include a return to the old social order in which men of this generation grew to maturity. The "good old days" have gone never to return. What follows will be much better or very much worse. Those days held their own tragedies, but for many of us they were very good, and memory tends to make them better. It bathes in its own rosy light the era of the horse and buggy and the kerosene lamp, an era over which we sentimentalize but to which we should most unwillingly return!

It is a commonplace statement of fact, yet an ever amazing source of wonder, that men fifty years of age and upward have seen in their own lifetime the entire development of the automobile, airplane, motion pictures and radio; and most of the development of the telephone and the electric light and power industry, as well as of the less conspicuous but equally revolutionary chemical industries. We have lived from the age of the Saturday night bath to the shower bath era; from the time when the housewife was scarcely respectable who did not put up her own fruit, if not her own vegetables, to the epoch whose coat of arms is the can-opener rampant.

I can remember vividly the first horseless carriage I ever saw and heard. It was propelled by a mixture of petroleum, profanity, and prayer down the few blocks of paved streets our town then boasted, its anxious owner more an object of laughter than of envy. Not many years ago, after a long absence, I drove in five or six minutes over well paved roads and relived in memory the long hours it had taken me on a dark summer night, caught in a sudden and violent storm, to cover that same distance behind my grandfather's old white horse, over a road deep in mud. Plumbing and central heating did not come to the dormitories of my own alma mater, Princeton, until after the turn of the century—in the summer, I think, of 1902.

My mother on her seventieth birthday remarked to her family that she doubted if in any seventy years of the past, or of the future, human beings would see such sweeping changes in the outward circumstances of life as she had witnessed. Her children's generation and her grandchildren's, if atomic energy should become available to the service of men, might dispute her claim. But no one would deny that the last hundred years have seen more changes in the way men live and do their work than in the thousands of years which preceded them since the dawn of civilization in the valleys of the Nile and the Euphrates. The physical conditions of our lives would have seemed little stranger to Moses than to George Washington.

It would have been a miracle if such profound changes in our way of living and of making a living had had no effect upon our political and economic system. The successful use of power-driven machinery has demanded specialization and integration of work. Collectively we have more because each of us does less; or to put it more accurately, and less epigrammatically, collectively we have more because most of us specialize in certain particular tasks, perhaps one process on a machine. This specialization applies not only to men as individuals, but to communities, none of which is self sufficient to the degree that all communities and the regions around them were self sufficient prior to the industrial revolution.

All of us are dependent every day of our lives on natural resources and great aggregations of machinery which cannot possibly be owned by us as individuals or even in small partnerships. Mr. Ralph Borsodi, to be sure, has made out an interesting case for decentralization, and the comparative self sufficiency of the family and community, on what might fairly be called the principle of "a Diesel engine in every home." It would by no means solve all the economic problems of the machine age, and it is completely out of line with the psychology of the denizens of the delicatessen belt who find their mass pleasures in motion picture theaters and baseball bleachers.

But of this, more later. Now we are concerned with remembering the days that are gone. It is easier to reconstruct the physical environment of our youth, despite the distortion and refraction of memory, than it is to recall again the world of our hopes and beliefs. Of one thing we are certain: the world of 1941 is a far darker place, more irrational and more bestially cruel than we could have believed in the years of hope which preceded the First World War.

It is an ironic fact, which does little to lighten the gloom, that the years of our progressive disillusionment have also been the years of achievement of most of the reforms which the followers, not only of Theodore Roosevelt, but even of Gene Debs, believed would set us a long way toward Utopia.

4

In 1925 and 1929, when I ran for Mayor of New York City, I set forth specifically and in detail our hopes and plans for making New York a better city. I said that the problem of our slums was insoluble without public housing. Mine was a voice crying in the wilderness, but even I, before the great depression, did not realize to what extent outright subsidy would be necessary to make that housing successful. I presented a rather elaborate program with regard to parks, playgrounds, and the like —and was soundly rebuked in a letter from one of New York's rich and public-spirited philanthropists for raising too great expectations. Thanks to Robert Moses, to unemployment, and to the necessity under private capitalism for putting men to work at jobs which do not compete with private business, that program has already been exceeded. Indeed when I consider how many proposals of the social workers, whose ranks I joined as a very green youngster in the fall of 1905, have since been fulfilled in New York City and the nation, I am divided between satisfaction over the achievement and disappointment that it has added so little to the sum of human happiness.

I have often tried, never too successfully, to put in words the difference between the world of my youthful expectations and my children's. Perhaps the matter can be summed up somewhat as follows: When the youth of my generation got through high school and college—to which, by the way, a smaller proportion went than now, partly because in those days one did not need a college diploma to clerk in Macy's—we expected to find jobs in a country free from war, in which progress onward and upward was the divine law of life.

It was good to be alive and young in the years between the turn of the century and the beginning of the First World War. On the whole, the country was prosperous and gaining in prosperity. The panic of 1907 was of short duration. Unemployment was far from unknown, but it was not a chronic and devastating disease. The average young man with reasonable health, reasonable energy, and reasonable luck was at least sure of a job. That we should live to see high school classes take as their motto "WPA, here we come" would have seemed incredible.

War, at any rate large-scale war between civilized nations, was a thing, we thought, of the backward past. True, the United States had recently dealt sternly with Spain, as God's agent in fulfillment of this country's own "manifest destiny." Minor wars were a regrettable necessity for the British Empire in dealing with those "lesser breeds without the law," over whom the Lord God of Hosts had given it dominion. Japan and Russia might clash in battle, but they were barely civilized, and the rôle of America toward them was that of peacemaker. We Americans pitied Europe for the costliness of its competitive armaments, but in a vague sort of way we thought preparedness made for peace rather than war, partly because modern war was so costly. Sober description of the nightly agony of bombing raids over great cities would have seemed to us the figment of a diseased imagination, a preposterous impossibility.

In this country we knew that many things were wrong and needed righting. We were aware of the horror of our lynchings and the violence of our strikes. Lincoln Steffens told us in vivid language of the shame of our cities and Jacob Riis and others had given us a sentimental interest in the fate of our slum dwellers. Reform and progress were in the air. The elder La Follette, the first Roosevelt, and Woodrow Wilson, each in his own way, were voluble in the support of social righteousness. Definitely the world was getting better, especially in our America. The devout Christian worked and hoped for "the evangelization of the world in this generation." The comparatively small group of Socialists year by year grew larger, and thousands of Gene Debs's loyal followers fully expected to live to march down Pennsylvania Avenue in his inaugural procession.

In those years of faith in "progress" theological fundamentalism was still strong, and in scores of communities evolution as a law of biology was frowned upon. But a well-nigh automatic process of social evolution toward a better world was tacitly accepted even by radicals who thought of themselves as revolutionary, and by religious believers in the doctrine of original sin. To us it seemed that mankind, at least in our own happy country, moved forward as on a ramp. It had only to keep going to reach ascending stages of well being. It could not lose its way. Exhortation was in order against shoving or loitering on the march. Scarcely more was necessary.

Idealism? Our youth had plenty of it. Usually it

found ways of doing good in connection with the church or social settlement or some reform organization. It had its brief delirium of battling at Armageddon for the Lord under the banners of Teddy Roosevelt.

Someone, I think, has called the years of which I write the Peter Pan Epoch of American history. Perhaps we did believe in fairies. Yet so real and generally desirable was that epoch to America's great middle class that its social institutions and viewpoints still in retrospect seem normal, something to which we may return after the long night of war and economic depression has passed.

Not even the Second World War has completely broken that hope. Those years before the First World War, the years of our youth, were the flowering of that "American way of life" whose praises now are so often on our lips. The hope of it sustained us through the First World War, again briefly in the Coolidge Epoch when, as William Allen White puts it, "a Puritan reigned in Babylon"; but there was a crasser material quality than in the days before the war when men swore allegiance to the spirit of progress. The later strength was the strength of fever and not of health.

The difficulty my generation has in understanding or in guiding the world of the Second Great War has been greatly increased by the failure of the revolution which has come upon us to conform to pattern. Modern totalitarianism was no part of the dream of the revolutionaries of the early twentieth century, whether or not they regarded themselves as Marxists. A considerable suspicion of the state was part of the American tradition; the anti-statism and syndicalism of the I.W.W., or Wobblies, was American to the core. American socialists generally assumed, in their controversies with capitalists on one hand and anarchists on the other, that the collectivism they advocated would be accompanied by an increase of true democracy; that their commonwealth would give freedom, as well as abundance, to a degree impossible under the capitalist state. Instead, collectivism in its various European forms has brought new, and in many respects worse, tyranny than it supplanted. Even in America, the trend is more toward the totalitarian state than the cooperative commonwealth. It thus becomes doubly easy for the men of my generation to tie democracy to private capitalism and to believe that they can live only if they live together.

Easy and natural, but dangerously erroneous.

The old order has irremediably failed to satisfy men's hopes and needs. That failure makes a new order inevitable, but by no means does it guarantee the moral quality of the new order. The Roman Empire fell largely because of its own internal weaknesses. It was doomed by its own mistakes. But so preferable was it to the Dark Ages that the children of its barbarian conquerors through long centuries looked back to the rule of the Empire which they had overthrown as to a Golden Era.

If our world is to escape its own spiritual dark ages, it cannot be by the preservation of the past which has already given birth to revolution.

9

CHAPTER II ☆ A FAILURE
IN LOYALTIES

IN PART, this book is a reappraisal of beliefs and hopes and plans which I have held and advocated for nearly a quarter of a century. But time and events have not forced me substantially to alter the convictions which made me turn to socialism.

Certainly I was not born or reared a socialist, nor was I suddenly converted by any one man, one book, or one event. It is because my youth was typical of so much of America that I refer to it briefly. I was born and reared in a happy home, in an environment genuinely religious and decidedly moralistic, eager for various reforms but almost unaware of socialism, or the reasons which made men socialists. My home town was none other than Marion, Ohio, the city of Warren Gamaliel Harding, who was later to become the pathetic symbol of a shameful and incredible era. Mr. Harding's home town—and mine—never got farther toward radicalism than to give, I think, a majority to William Jennings Bryan in 1896. I was graduated from Princeton University, the Princeton of a Woodrow Wilson who had by no means then formulated "the New Freedom"—which Princeton never enthusiastically accepted. I studied socialism under a professor who never thought it necessary to have us read any of the socialist classics, but only criticisms of them, and for some years after my graduation, even when I was engaged in social and church work in New York

City, I hoped to write a book refuting socialism in favor of a reformed capitalism.

Two things gradually made me a socialist. First, personal experience in the poorer parts of New York City, which convinced me that in an important sense our various reform efforts were, in the words of the familiar simile, like bailing out a tub while we kept the faucet running; and second, the World War, which I came to believe was an imperialist struggle, to be accounted for in terms of the socialist analysis.

From the beginning of my experience as a socialist I was convinced of a fundamental truth which I have since formulated scores of times in speech and writing somewhat as follows: Our familiar social order has been failing because of the inadequacy of its basic loyalties and the institutions connected with, and inspired by, them.

Men and societies live by their loyalties. Selfishness is a human fault which impedes social progress, but rarely is a man so egoistic but that he has some group loyalty. The Scotchman of the celebrated prayer, "God bless me and my wife, my son John and his wife, us four and no more" reduced his group loyalty to about the narrowest possible terms, but it was still a group loyalty. Historically, men have been loyal to such diverse groupings as the clan, the patriarchical family, the city-state, the church, and the complex of personal relationships which constituted the feudal system.

The average modern American has a bewildering and often contradictory set of loyalties; family, church, trade union, Chamber of Commerce, lodge, civic society, etc. That is one of the important facts of our times. But modern man's *major* loyalties have been two: (1) the absolute national state, and (2) the profit system or private capitalism. These two dominant loyalties began to emerge with the Renaissance and the Protestant Reformation; they achieved the mastery of the world with the French Revolution, and they dominated human history down to the First World War. The competitive imperialisms born of them were directly responsible for the First World War. Of those competitive imperialisms, the oldest, the strongest, and the most typical, has been British.

The concept of nationalism was at once more unifying and more divisive than were the dominant loyalties of the Middle Ages. More unifying by contrast with the ideals and social institutions of feudalism. The France of the great days of the House of Bourbon was a unit in a sense in which the France of the great duchies, whose rivalries had made possible one hundred years of aggression by the British kings, never could be. But the loyalties of that nationalism which first came to flower in England and France made men far less good Europeans than they had been in Roman times, in the years when Charlemagne briefly made his Roman Empire a new reality, or even in the centuries when the Empire lived as a shadowy concept alongside the great reality of the one Roman Catholic Church to which the whole western world belonged.

Upon what might have happened if the rise of national states, accompanied by the religion of patriotism, had conformed to economic realities, it is idle to speculate. It did not happen.

At the time of the First World War, only the United States of America approximated potential economic self sufficiency. The vast Russian Empire had the requisite natural resources, but was very backward industrially. England and France were largely dependent on widely scattered empires which had been acquired out of desire for markets abroad, for sources of supply of raw materials, and for opportunities for the investment of surplus capital. (The dominance of these desires did not exclude desire for glory, plain accident, and, in the case of the English, the need for opportunities for younger sons to exercise their talents. All these contributed to the growth of Empire.)

Despite the indissoluble relationship between nationalism and capitalism in the modern world, the logic of the two was in part contradictory. Capitalism in its pure theory depended upon free trade, not only within each nation, but internationally. That sort of trade was greatly impeded by the pressure of national interests. Foreign trade has always been and always will be a condition of the highest prosperity. It was, and is, the condition of life for the smaller nations. Yet only Great Britain, from the repeal of the Corn Laws until well within the twentieth century, was loyal to free trade between nations. And the British revolt against the eighteenth century mercantilism was stimulated not only by the loss of the American Colonies, but by the fact that the industrial revolution, and with it modern capitalism, had gained an immense head start in England. Free trade, therefore, suited British national interest as well as the logic of capitalism. When it no longer suited that interest it was abandoned.

What has steadily widened the gulf between a rational economic order and nationalism is the historic fact that nationalism has always found its highest expression in war. Trade has never been considered on the basis of a calm interest of peoples in an order of continuing peace. Always there has been the fear, based on grim experience, that a nation might be deprived of supplies from outside its borders not only by the fortunes of its own wars, but by the power of its belligerent neighbors. Since this fear never brought with it the wisdom to end the war system, it enormously sharpened the rivalry of the stronger, more fortunate nations for imperial advantage, and led straight to the wastes and distortions of the economic order which competitive militarism must impose. Thus has their supreme loyalty to nationalism driven the peoples along the road whose end has been the second world war in one generation.

Capitalism has had its own peculiar share in bringing modern wars to birth. Its failure even here in the United States is, as I believe, the principal element in our American turn to armament economics and imperialism which sooner or later means war. But the system's failure is most immediately and obviously made apparent to the common man by the insecurity under which he suffers, and the poverty of which he is a victim. Year by year he has become aware that, given the advance in modern technology, this poverty is more and more unnecessary. But private capitalism of its own volition offers no cure. Hence in every country there is compelling pressure upon the state to intervene in that economic process whose glory it was, according to its priests and pundits, that it was automatic and required no state intervention to bring about the maximum satisfaction of human needs.

If Adam Smith, whose *Wealth of Nations* appeared in the same year as our Declaration of Independence, had made a tour of the world in the summer before the outbreak of the Second World War, he would have been amazed to find how far that world had departed from the principles which seemed indispensable to the first interpreter of capitalism. He might have been more astonished to find how far state intervention in the economic order had gone in his own country under a Tory government, nominally devoted to the maintenance of the profit system, than by the fate of that system in the totalitarian lands, or the democratic and semi-socialist societies of the Scandinavian countries and New Zealand. But as a wise man he would have come to the conclusion that the reasons for state intervention in the economic order were so compelling that they forced themselves on all governments despite the varying economic and political theories over which men quarrelled.

The Second World War has completed the downfall of the old capitalism. With England fighting for her life, Ernest Bevin, the dominant figure in the Labor Party, paused to proclaim that Europe is going through a revolutionary process which the next peace settlement must acknowledge and deal with; and that his own England must recognize that the masses of men desire a security which the old order did not give them. (But neither he nor his party has yet implemented their general assertions by a vital program.)

Only in the United States is faith in the older capitalism still strong, and only here does the going economic order bear a recognizable relation to the economic theories of private capitalism. Yet even in America, the land whose history and geography gave it the best chance to solve the problem of poverty, its failure has been attested less by the electoral triumphs of Mr. Roosevelt than by the admission of that crusader for so much as can be saved of the old order, Wendell L. Willkie, that he would accept in principle every form of state intervention which his rival has sponsored.

When Mr. Willkie so emphatically endorsed all the reforms which President Roosevelt had appropriated from Socialist immediate demands, he did not, of course, endorse socialism or any adequate cure for insecurity and our wholly unnecessary poverty. But he did unconsciously betray the capitalism or private profit system in which he trusts. For the genius of that system lay precisely in its repudiation of such state intervention as Mr. Willkie supports. Indeed, Von Mises, its theoretical champion, regards such intervention, mistakenly, as "socialism." Certainly it is a repudiation of the "automatic equilibrium of markets," and it requires a new economic justification going far beyond Mr. Willkie's assertion that his system was necessary to democracy, and, with these uncongenial reforms, would work if somehow "confidence" could be restored by his election. The reforms that under one administration led to destruction could hardly be the means of salvation under another ruler!

Most of all, the failure of private capitalism is attested by the grim facts of daily life. The United States, prior to its swing into the dangerous expansion of armament economics, was becoming used to a standing army of the unemployed averaging ten million workers. In February 1940 according to the survey of conditions in *Fortune*, 23 per cent, almost a quarter of our entire population, were wholly outside the going economic order. They lived on public and private relief and "made work," with now and then some casual and ill-requited employment. They could disappear entirely from the economic scene and in the economic sense they would not be missed except as they would reduce the market for subsistence goods. A Congressional Committee investigating migratory workers in 1940, in a preliminary statement by its chairman, set their number at four million souls, about evenly divided between workers with an agricultural and with an industrial background.

Before the armament boom in the same year (1940) two-thirds of the families of America received less than $1,500 in annual family income. An income of $1,500 is just a shade above the usual estimate of a minimum budget of health and decency for the family of five.

Fifty-five per cent of our people receive family incomes less than $1,250, which is the minimum budget of health and decency for a family of four under urban conditions. Ten per cent receive less than $300 annually. John L. Lewis's rhetorical reference to "fifty-two million pinched bellies" is less exaggerated than the physically comfortable but mentally worried members of the middle class may realize.

What makes this situation intolerable to the individuals who suffer under it—and makes it a threat to our social order—is the recognized fact that we have everything we need except good sense to produce abundance. Mr. Willkie himself in his post-election speech referred to an immediately possible national income of 100 billion dollars.

Various economists have raised Mr. Willkie's estimate of 100 billion dollars as the immediately attainable national income by ten or even twenty-five billion dollars annually. Hence $2,500 a year with our present technological equipment might easily be a minimum income for every family worth holding together at all without any drastic reduction of higher incomes—except as national defense will alter this picture.

The failure of our system to use its machinery effectively for the common good is dramatically emphasized by the methods we have felt compelled to adopt in our struggle against long continued depression. Thus, in a country where a well-fed population would require much more food, we are subsidizing farmers not to produce so much, and our first attack upon surplus cotton was to reduce the cotton acreage, not to see that the children of the men who raise it are decently clad.

The evidence of the failure of private capitalism does not, of course, automatically establish the case for socialism or any other system; it does render worse than dubious the passionate but ill-defined faith of the upper and middle classes in the United States that a mere change in the personnel of government and a more sympathetic attitude to business would make their beloved system work in the next decade as satisfactorily as it worked prior to the First World War, or—as they think —in the Harding and Coolidge epoch. It will not.

As matters now stand, their hope will never be tried out, for the United States has turned to an armament economics which will impose its own inexorable logic upon the country. And that logic in our day is not the logic of a successful and prosperous private capitalism even though under it, for a time, private profits for the fortunate will be kept, and probably greatly enhanced.

In earlier books I have analyzed the reasons for the failure of private capitalism, and its present dangerous inadequacy as one of the major organizing principles of society. I shall not repeat that analysis here, but I shall emphasize certain features of it, especially those which have been forcibly impressed upon us by the rapidity of private capitalism's descent toward the limbo of old social systems.*

* Out of the extensive literature, I want to recommend for facts and their objective interpretation, National Resources Committee: *The Structure of the American Economy*, Washington 1939; E. D. Kennedy: *Dividends to Pay* (Reynal and Hitchcock); John Blair: *Seeds of De-*

The period of capitalist expansion was a period of rapid increase of population not only among industrially backward peoples but also in the leading capitalist nations themselves. The population of the world in 1800, about the time when Malthus uttered his despairing prophecy that mankind was dooming itself to inexorable starvation by the rate of its own increase, was 836,000,-000. In 1933 it was 2,057,000,000 according to the figures cited and accepted by Carr-Saunders in his book *World Population*. Yet the United States, which had been helping to feed Europe before the war, was artificially reducing its production of foodstuffs! So far were the Malthusian prophecies from fulfillment!

Not only had the world not failed in production as Malthus had expected; it had also begun drastically to slow up its rate of increase, especially in the more advanced nations. The change in the rate of increase is by no means uniform but is most marked in the "Have" nations. In a new country like the United States it is probably only a matter of two or three decades before our population will be stationary. In five years the number of women will, for the first time in our history, begin to pass the number of men.

In at least two respects this slowing up of the rate of increase in population is significant for the economic order. In the first place, the rapid increase of population during the nineteenth century created a steadily increas-

struction (Covici-Friede); Beard and Smith: *The Old Deal and the New* (Macmillan). With the last named in the field of analysis I am in hearty agreement at all important points except that I regret some omissions.

ing demand for subsistence goods, a demand which even panic could not abolish. Markets for subsistence goods, and their expansion with an increasing population, do not require the creative intelligence and forethought which are necessary for the anticipation and supplying of human wants far beyond the subsistence level. Yet it is upon this new kind of economic enterprise, steadily maintained without recurring depression, that our prosperity will increasingly depend. Farmers to whom the industrial revolution came late have been peculiarly victims of the decline in the rate of increase of our population.

A second characteristic of the population situation in the western nations is a shift in the dominant age group. The America of pioneer days, the America of great immigration, was a young man's country. It is becoming a country of the middle aged because of decreasing birth rate, exclusion of immigration, and increasing longevity (according to the census of 1940 the median age in America had risen to twenty-nine) on which the organized political pressure of the dissatisfied "elder citizens" is a growing force. Unless the United States can greatly increase production we shall see a new class war between the young and the old to govern the direction of state intervention in the distribution of an inadequate income. Indeed it has already begun in states like Colorado which have sacrificed education to the effort to pay larger old age pensions. More than that, the psychology of middle age, and still more of the older years, is not the psychology which characterized the growth of our nation. It is the psychology to which security seems the highest good. And security is by no means synonymous with democracy.

Perhaps the most ominous of all the consequences of this decline in the birth rate of the western nations, so long as they persist in their habits of war, may be a tragic reduction in constructive power. They may, sooner than they think, reach a point where they cannot maintain their natural existence, and this not only because of the physical slaughter of the young men who are always first in war, but because of other less immediate biological effects upon the well-being of those whose youth has been blighted by destruction.

A second change in our world is the disappearance of the frontier. It is superfluous to dwell upon the deep significance of a fact which has already aroused so much discussion. There is, however, one aspect of it which is worth a passing word. Not only has the physical frontier disappeared in the United States, and, to a less degree, in other regions of the temperate zone, but in a machine age the psychology of the frontiersman has almost vanished. All land and resources are now "owned" by men, groups and nations. They are not to be had by discovery and use. Colonization is now an elaborate and costly enterprise. Men have to be driven to it by political persecution or economic desperation. Witness the Jewish settlements in Palestine, or the none too successful attempt of our own government to establish a small colony in Alaska. And, worst of all, the heartbreaking failure of the well-intentioned foes of fascism to promote any extensive resettlement of war's victims, even in sparsely populated lands. Here the difficulties arise not only from the psychology of the victims but even more from the nationalism of all the governments concerned. There is today virtually no escape at "the end of the wilderness trail" for "rugged individuals" who are discontented with their political and economic environment.

Other changes too obvious and too often discussed to need elaboration here include the continual improvement of machines and technological processes, the increasing proportion of workers not directly engaged in production, and the tendency for an increasing part of the consumer's dollar to be absorbed in distribution.

Private capitalism under the impact of these external changes, and as a result of its own internal contradictions, has changed its own quality. It has developed irresponsible absentee ownership on a widespread scale through the devices of stockholding in great corporations. These corporations are "persons" under the law, but persons with only one function, and that to make profit. They are permitted by law and by custom no other activity than that which may help them make profits. Contributions to charitable ends can be justified only on the ground that they contribute to good will and hence to profit. To grant better wages and working conditions to workers is permissible only under pressure of the workers' own organizations, or to forestall unionization, or to increase satisfaction, and hence production and profit. In capitalist theory the masses would achieve their maximum well-being if these inhuman corporate "persons" thus made profit. It hasn't happened that way. The first effect of the New Deal was actually to increase monopolistic tendencies and the supremacy of great corporations through NRA. The code authorities set up while the Blue Eagle was still flying high were, in general, dominated by the representatives of larger business interests at the time when the Supreme Court, probably to President Roosevelt's secret relief, wiped out an experiment whose benefits had been confined to a short initial period. The administration turned to a new version of the opposite policy of "trust busting" under Thurman Arnold. It has not gone far enough greatly to alter the picture under which the two hundred largest corporations control half of the business wealth of the country, and the chances are that both trust-busting, under the present law, and the attempt of Congress and the administration to write new laws as a result of the findings of the Temporary National Economic Commission, will be virtually suspended for an indefinite period in the interest of harmonious cooperation in armament economics.

Even nations unwilling to admit that the developments of a machine age require a large element of socialist planning properly to supply man's peacetime wants, admit its necessity for war and preparation for war. In the long run, armament economics will destroy the private capitalism which turns to it as the only form of expansion which it understands. But we are still living in the early stage of a program likely to employ idle money and idle men to the temporary profit of a powerful class of private owners, but under social direction. This same idle money and these same idle men have not been employed for the last decade under the initiative of that desire for profit which to the older capitalist apologists was the all-sufficient drive for expansion.

Why not? Partly because well established enterprises, especially as they approach monopolistic control, are more concerned with protecting what they have than with general business expansion. For that protection they are even willing or eager to accept some government intervention; e.g., through tariffs and price codes of the old NRA, which they will not accept for the promotion of new enterprises.

The last decade's paralysis of capitalist expansion seems to be having a curious psychological effect. Apparently it is bringing about a return to the psychology of hoarding. For hundreds of years it was the natural tendency of the man with extra money to hoard it in the form of gold and jewels. Such precious materials represent much of the wealth of the Indian princes to this day. It was a basic assumption of the economic theory of my youth that wealth, under the capitalist system, could not and would not be hoarded by its possessors. The volume of idle money in our banks has seemed to give the lie to that complacent theory. Wealth today is cautious, not adventurous; and the fault is not all President Roosevelt's!

All these facts taken together seem to me to establish an overwhelming case for the inadequacy of zeal for private profit in providing steam to make our marvellous productive engine go. Clearly, after some fashion we must substitute for it a social purpose; that is, a deliberate intention to produce what men want and need, for which production we already have the resources and machinery.

This is not to say that always and everywhere bigness in the machine age is a virtue, or that there is no place for any sort of competition. It is to say that events bear out what an analysis of the machine age suggests; namely, the necessity of social purpose and plan for the effective use of the technological resources of an age whose maximum production depends upon integration and specialization. In other words, our brief examination strengthens the conclusion that we cannot cure our insecurity and unnecessary poverty by trying to go back to the economics of the horse-and-buggy age in the era of automobile assembly lines.

The danger is that we shall work out an economics appropriate to the assembly line primarily for the production of armaments which, whatever their seeming necessity, have no economic value whatever. Germany under the Nazis has done a marvellous job technologically, for horrible ends. Hitler took control of a country still smarting under defeat in a great war, a country where unemployment was terrific, natural resources few, and gold and international credit entirely lacking. In a pragmatic sort of way, inspired by a grim purpose, Hitler and his technicians in seven short years managed to cut a vast amount of economic red tape and put Germany's skilled workers and excellent machinery directly to the task of producing the military machine which conquered most of Europe. However destructive Hitler's immediate purpose, however surely he has doomed the ultimate power of his own Germany by the intolerance which has put her greatest scientists and thinkers to death or into exile, he has proved once and for all that social purpose and social planning can successfully accomplish prodigious results.

True, lack of resources has compelled Germany to choose to a marked degree between guns and butter. Her people have been more easily persuaded to accept guns in the hope of ultimately winning more butter, that is more of the riches of a world in which she has felt she has not had her share. Our country may not have to make so sharp a choice between guns and butter, nor do we have so definite a material urge to conquest, but I can see no reason to believe that we shall be much more successful than Germany in making true prosperity a by-product of armament economics. And I am far from sure that we shall be as successful in the technical application of social control for purposes of what is euphemistically called "defense."

At any rate, unless in our American way of life there is developed a new and conscious loyalty to the conquest of poverty, the movement will be in the direction of our type of fascism, not democracy; of our own totalitarian state and not a cooperative commonwealth. But to establish this contention will require an examination of recent history, and especially of the wars which have marked Europe's confused and ugly revolution. To that we now turn.

CHAPTER III ☆ TWO WORLD WARS

TO THE majority of Americans in 1917 the First World War which they had entered was "a war to end war" and "to make the world safe for democracy." The German Kaiser was the Beast of Berlin and the enemy of God and man.

To the great majority of Americans in 1937, however, the First World War seemed an imperialist conflict, not fought for ideal ends, into which we had been fooled by propaganda and coerced by economic pressures. The Kaiser was a harmless exile in Doorn who in the retrospect compared tolerably well with most world rulers, and was positively beneficent by contrast to his successor, Adolf Hitler.

In 1940 there was another shift in public opinion, and many Americans were ready to agree with President Roosevelt's Armistice Day speech at the Tomb of the Unknown Soldier that the war had been a necessary answer to Germany's first challenge to democracy, and that American participation in it was praiseworthy.

So impermanent are historical judgments, and so surely is history not a science of truth but part of the ritual of patriotism, ministering to the present needs of the national state!

Nevertheless, the judgment of most historians and the majority of the people in the years before the renewal of the conflict was factually correct. Debate may be in order about degrees of guilt for the First World War, but none of the nations involved in its outbreak can escape some responsibility for it. The war was a conflict of rival imperialisms, not a strife between light and darkness. It was a proof of the failure of the old order and its loyalties. And it hastened the revolutionary processes and made them more violent and cruel. It took Woodrow Wilson's eloquence to make it a war for democracy.

In the disillusionment of Americans who came to feel that they got nothing out of the war except great debts which they could not collect from the borrowers, and who saw that their victory had not made the world safe for democracy, for peace, or even for common decency, it was easy to oversimplify and personalize the economic pressures which had driven us into the war. The House of Morgan was probably made the villain to a degree beyond its deserts. Yet all the discussion of the years has given me no reason to alter materially the conclusion which I reached in 1917, a conclusion substantiated by books like Walter Millis's *Road to War*, and the long investigations of the Nye Committee of the United States Senate. The causes of the war were not simple. British propaganda and the undeniable crimes of the Germans played their part, but we should not have got into the war as active belligerents if our whole economy had not been increasingly tied in to the service of the Allies, and if farmers and workers, as well as the House of Morgan, had not acquired an economic stake in Allied victory. Individual men with great sincerity fought for democracy, but the economic forces which President

Wilson admitted in his famous St. Louis speech were responsible for the war, were also responsible for American entry into it.

If America as a nation had had an intelligent interest in peace and democracy the government would have used its moral and economic power to bring about a negotiated peace. The right sort of mediation might have brought about a negotiated peace on several occasions before Woodrow Wilson put us into the war which he had hoped to avoid without knowing how. One of those opportunities for peace came as early as the first winter of the war after the German drive on Paris had been checked and the Russian drive against Germany had been repulsed. That first Christmas in the trenches fraternizing between the lines was general.

A negotiated peace would have been far from perfect. It would not have stopped the processes of the decay of the old order or the coming of a new order to birth. It might have made those processes less brutal and catastrophic. We might have avoided a Hitler, a Mussolini, a Stalin, or their equivalent.

What might have been is food for conjecture, but conjecture which has meaning for our own day. What was we know all too well. The First World War, the Peace of Versailles, and the years which followed paved the way for the Second World War. This war also is imperialist in its origin, in a sense a renewal of the first. But definitely on a far worse plane. The imperialisms of 1914, certainly the British, the French and the German, shared a common economics and a common culture. It was the culture of liberal capitalism and political democracy. The German manner was more militaristic and its governmental institutions less democratic than the French or British, but liberty for minority groups and individual critics of the régime was about as well protected in Germany as in England and France. Under the Kaiser the Socialist Party was not even driven underground, much less ruthlessly destroyed. The Kaiser was personally friendly to prominent Jews; it was the Russian Empire, ally of the democracies, which was anti-Semitic.

Nothing of the sort is true in the Second World War.* The Axis powers are contemptuously anti-Semitic and anti-democratic. They have employed brutal cruelty as an instrument of government in a way to shock the conscience of the older imperialisms, internally more or less democratic at home, and inclined to forget or overlook the ruthless cruelty they have long used to impose and maintain their sway over the colored races of Africa, Asia and America.

The economy of the new imperialism is different from the old, and so is its form of political organization. In the fascist countries, private capitalism has given way to state capitalism, and the more or less liberal democratic state has been replaced by the totalitarian rule of a dicta-

---

* The old socialist absolutism concerning the similarity of all wars and all armaments therefore needs modification. There are differences. Unless one is an absolute pacifist, one can oppose *all* military defense only if one believes all nations about equally good or bad, or if one believes that war will result in a general revolution against it on both sides. My case against our involvement in this war, and against armament economics, is based on less absolute considerations.

tor and the party of which he is the leader. Hence while the Second World War is not a struggle for democracy—rather today it is being fought by the British for the life of their nation and their Empire—nevertheless a partial democracy and the whole liberal culture that we had falsely come to believe was the normal possession of the European peoples are involved in the outcome. The First World War hastened a European revolution uglier in many of its aspects than any revolutionaries, prior to the advent of the totalitarian state, fascist or communist, anticipated. The Second World War in an important sense is bound up with that revolution. It has so far hastened it that even the most sweeping British victory could not restore the boundaries of 1937, or the familiar British way of life with its mingled good and evil, or maintain on the old familiar terms the British Empire— a basic fact more generally recognized in England than in America. Indeed, a very considerable part of American support for England comes less from love of democracy, or even from ties of blood and language and respect for gallant resistance to invasion, than from identification of Great Britain and the British Empire with private capitalism the world around and hence with one version of the American way of life. (See, for instance, Wendell Willkie's remarks at the Town Meeting of the Air Jan. 20, 1940, as published in its Bulletin). Because they believe that private capitalism can somehow be saved by British victory large sections of the upper and middle classes are willing, if necessary, to put America into war for it. But even to themselves they usually call

32

it "war for democracy" and they completely fail to understand that by war all they can do is to hasten the doom of the economic order they love.

These are strong statements. They can best be supported by a brief examination of events since the First World War.

The victory of nations ostensibly pledged to democracy in the First World War, and the Russian Revolution during it, on the face of things should have given mankind, and especially the European portion of it, an unparalleled opportunity to establish a social order to which peace might be appropriate. The opportunity was lost.

Mr. Archibald MacLeish has attracted wide attention by his eloquent lamentation that the writers and intellectuals of his generation gave to modern youth a too sweeping and indiscriminate hatred of war. Whether Mr. MacLeish is right or wrong in his judgment is beside my present point. His lamentations are not a confession of the primary sin or failure of the leaders of his generation and mine. What we should repent in sackcloth and ashes is the stupidity or the weakness which made us so impotent to organize a world fit for peace and freedom during the period between the Armistice and Hitler's access to power when that task would have been relatively easier than it will be again for weary years if not for generations. The men of our generation failed because they neither understood nor would willingly pay the price of peace.

At the time of the signing of the Peace of Versailles,

33

the *New York Call,* a Socialist publication, printed a prophetic cartoon. Around a table in a marble hall old men were signing the treaty; half hidden behind a column a little child was weeping and the child was labelled "Class of 1940." The Peace of Versailles was indeed a peace to end peace and to sentence the youth of 1940 to war. It is quite likely—and beside the point—that the Kaiser in the event of equally sweeping victory would have imposed worse terms, as he did on the Russians at Brest-Litovsk. It is possible to find many excuses for the peacemakers. The mistakes of Versailles were not peculiar to "the old men" who were made the scapegoats by many liberal and Leftist writers. They were the mistakes natural to the system which the people still accepted, and to the attitude of mind which attends victory after an exhausting war. Lloyd George deliberately perpetuated his power by shrewd timing of a "hang the Kaiser" general election. But if he was guilty of an unworthy bit of demagoguery, and a cynical appeal to a thirst for vengeance which he did not expect to gratify, certainly the voters who responded to that appeal were not innocent.

The great mistakes of Versailles were these: the Treaty created an impossible economic situation by its reparations sections; it gave future German agitators well grounded grievances to exploit; and it added to the disorganization of Europe—that disorganization which from the time when Charlemagne divided his empire among his sons had been so fruitful of wars. The principle of self-determination of nations was applied where it would help the victors and not otherwise. As the *sole* principle of the reorganization of continental Europe, the self-determination of nations, each of which claimed absolute sovereignity, was positively dangerous. Twenty-six absolutely sovereign states of uneven size and strength in Europe west of Russia, an area two-thirds the size of the United States, was in itself the negation of prosperity or peace.* To be valuable or permanent, self-determination in the crazy-quilt of European nationalities had to be supplemented by some sort of federation, otherwise it was inevitable that the strife for European or regional hegemony would go on.

Woodrow Wilson and his followers thought that the League of Nations would be a sufficient principle of federation and a means for the orderly correction of the mistakes of Versailles. They were gravely in error. A sound federation depends upon a positive cooperation between the federated peoples to get things done for their mutual well being. It cannot possibly depend merely upon agreement to coerce the evil doer. While there were positive types of cooperation set up under the League in connection with the Labor Office and certain machinery for social reform, in vital political matters each state was left sovereign. The only provision for cooperation as against coercion was in Article Nineteen which provided for League initiative in the revision of treaties, and that article was from the beginning a dead letter. Not only was the League as thus set up no compensation for the bad concessions which President Wil-

* Twenty-seven if tiny Lichtenstein is counted as well as Luxemburg.

son permitted at Versailles; it was in itself so tied up with old loyalties of capitalist-nationalism that it could not become even a beginning of a sound and hopeful world federation.

We American Socialists saw this after a fashion in 1918–1919; hence we opposed America's entering into the League. We did not believe that the America of the post-war reaction, the America of Warren G. Harding and the rising Ku Klux Klan, had any wisdom to contribute to Europe, and we did not wish to see America's physical strength wasted in enforcing the provisions of the Treaty of Versailles amid Europe's confusions. Nevertheless, I am the only Presidential candidate of any party who after 1920 advocated American entry into the League on any terms. This I did without great enthusiasm in 1928 and 1932 in accordance with the Socialist Platform of those years. We then felt after the admission of Germany to the League council, and the temporary improvements in Europe under the leadership of Briand and Stresemann that there was a chance, under certain conditions which were not fulfilled, for the United States to become a useful member of the League. By 1936, however, we believed that that chance had been lost and that to join the League would be in effect for the United States to become an ally of Tory Britain in the new war which then seemed all too likely. This Socialist record is not one which I should substantially alter.

British and French policy following Versailles was to maintain their own empires and their own commanding position at the cheapest possible cost. That meant maintaining the disorganization of Europe which had been so great an aid to Britain's easy acquisition of empire. It soon came to mean opposition to the revolutionary forces of communism and fascism. But the ruling groups and classes in both France and England, more especially England, misjudged fascism and temporized with it in an effort to use it against communism. Indeed, from Versailles on, although both the victors in the First World War understood the necessity of common action, there were wide differences of opinion between Whitehall and the Quai d'Orsay concerning the time to be firm and the time to be conciliatory to Germany. British public opinion and policy were usually more pro-German than were the French, yet it was a French statesman, Aristide Briand, who, together with the German, Gustav Stresemann, came the nearest to establishing the peace of Europe. But they were never able to act soon enough or drastically enough to build on foundations of political and economic cooperation a structure of European peace. The victorious Allies continued to prepare the way for Hitler's triumph by the occupation of the Ruhr, the refusal to permit a customs union between Germany and Austria, the complete failure to disarm themselves as they had promised to do in the treaty which disarmed Germany, and their blundering handling of reparations and other economic problems.

Conceivably, they might have preserved their own position and kept a peace which both of them desired by one of two policies: frank conciliation with Germany and cooperation in the reorganization of Europe, at least west of the Russian boundary; or a firm maintenance of military supremacy over a disarmed Germany. The latter would have required a more military spirit and perhaps an easier conscience than either England or France possessed. Logically, it would have demanded of the French a higher birth rate and of the English an earlier willingness to adopt military conscription. Whatever the reasons, no clear-cut policy was ever adopted. The fascism which, both in Italy and Germany, sprang in part out of resentment against the Treaty of Versailles and British and French dominance, was actually nurtured by both countries. Professor Salvemini has told us how Mussolini was saved in his early days of power by Wall Street loans and the friendship of the British Foreign Office. The French armament trust contributed to Hitler's war chest during his struggle for power. Mussolini would scarcely have dared even to plan the conquest of Ethiopia against vigorous and unified British and French opposition. The same sort of opposition might have prevented the beginning of the Franco revolution which was instead encouraged by British capitalist interests in Spain. Indeed, the completely hypocritical policy of "non-intervention" for which the British Tory government must assume primary blame bore a definite and positive responsibility for the defeat of the Loyalists. The British and French governments virtually encouraged Hitler to use Spain as the guinea pig on which to develop the new tactics of mechanized warfare.

The United States, whose responsibility toward Europe was far less than the British or French, never did what ideally it might have done, in or out of the League, to help in the establishment of prosperity and peace. When President Hoover signed the Smoot-Hawley bill still further increasing the already high American tariffs, he added to Europe's economic difficulties and helped to nullify his own efforts for reduction of armaments. When President Roosevelt slavishly followed British policy in dealing with Spain he helped to aid that fascism which he fears and hates. He could not plead in his own defense that any other policy might have involved his country in war. An embargo which only hurt Loyalist Spain was not necessary to our peace; still less was it necessary to our peace to ignore the fact that Italy and Germany were waging actual war on Spain and to refuse to apply the provisions of the Neutrality Law of 1937 against them.

An American Socialist who in 1918 and 1919 expressed as little hope as I did of the ability of the victorious governments to make a lasting peace, and as much hope as I did that the socialist movement of Europe might succeed where governments failed, cannot honestly put the whole blame for new world war upon the statesmen who wrote so sorry a record in the history of the years between the two great conflicts. The socialists of Europe also failed. The great Social Democratic Party of Germany had its day of opportunity when the Kaiser fled from his defeated Reich. To a less degree, the socialists in Italy and the smaller nations of Central

Europe had their chance. No group of them was able to take it. Today the Second International of Socialists and Workers, the body which boasted its adherents in every land, the organization which had dared to talk and dream of stopping war and remaking civilization, is broken. Its leaders are dead, imprisoned and in exile. The movement of Marx and Engels, of Bebel, Jaurès and Matteoti, is proscribed, driven underground, liquidated altogether, in practically all of Europe. Only in Great Britain is it strong.

Some of the reasons for the tragic failure of organized socialism in its day of opportunity are obvious and well agreed upon by socialists and non-socialists. In the confused days following the armistice, socialist action in various countries was on national lines. It was not synchronized; it was defeated in detail. In Germany socialists had a well-grounded fear of the Allies if they should push their socialism aggressively; in any event, they had no constructive program. They trusted too much to a socialist evolution under a liberal political constitution. Almost everywhere the bitterness of division between socialists and communists was fatal to the success of either.

To these reasons I am now inclined to add another, which I have given before, but which today I would emphasize: The physical and biological consequence of long continued warfare is fatal to the sustained creative energy necessary to establish a democratic socialism. Just as the Peloponnesian War was death to "the glory that was Greece," so will continuance of war, of itself, bring death to modern European civilization. No nobility of purpose or hope can alter that fact.

Furthermore, I am constrained to admit that the failure of socialism in the form of social democracy, together with the evolution of Stalinism out of Leninism in the U.S.S.R. suggests certain basic shortcomings or defects in Marxism itself if not in socialism. Before German dominance over the Scandinavian countries, socialism had done its best in those northern lands which were comparatively little disturbed by the dialectics of orthodox Marxism. The British Labor Party, today the only powerful socialist force in western Europe, is also not Marxist.

Of course it does not follow that a force of such tremendous and hopeful significance as Marxist socialism is dead. Further discussion of certain respects in which I question its adequacy, either as science or religion, must await a later stage of this book. But it requires no long argument to substantiate the charge that, in a time of revolutionary change, the working class of Europe did not play the rôle expected of it by Marxian socialists. That fact is attested not only by the failure of social democracy on the Continent, but by the lamentable evolution of communism into totalitarianism and the rise of fascism.

I have dwelt on the history of fascism and communism in other books; I need not repeat it here. I am compelled, to my profound regret, to modify my judgment in the case of communism for the worse. In the case of both fascism and communism I should put

41

greater emphasis on their growing resemblances. Despite the fact that fascism, both in its Italian and its German form, began with violent opposition to communism, despite the possibility that they may yet be rivals for world empire, they are similar in that they present a perversion of social revolution into a totalitarian form. Both of them developed out of the failure of the old order which called itself democratic. Both of them use the same tactic of propaganda unrestrained by truth, and terrorism untempered by mercy. Both of them exalt the mass at the expense of the individual. Originally, in communist theory, the sacred mass was the working class, international in its extent. Practically, Stalin has gone far to make the Russian nation a sacred entity although he still clings to some vestiges of theoretical internationalism, and has the support of an international communist movement. The sacred books of communism are far nobler in respect to breadth of vision than *Mein Kampf*. From the beginning it was the nation, and not only the nation but the nation *conceived in tribal terms*, which was sacred to Hitler. He cunningly transferred to "the proletarian nation" the feelings of resentment and the struggle for power which Marxism assigned to a proletarian class which ignored national lines.

Both communism and fascism, however hateful in many of their aspects, are revolutionary forces, part of the same cycle of war-revolution-war. This revolutionary quality of fascism I was long inclined to deny. I never accepted the definition of fascism once popular in Leftist circles as "capitalism with its mask off." I used to insist that it was "capitalism with a new mask on." In its development—particularly in Germany, which rather than Italy is the real seat of its strength—fascism is not capitalist at all, certainly not in the sense in which capitalism is understood by its orthodox economists and apologists. Neither is "national socialism" truly socialist in the sense in which any of the great socialist propagandists of the Right or of the Left understood socialism.

But the same thing can be said of the Russian economic order. Certainly the workers are as far removed in Russia as in Germany from real ownership or control of the great aggregations of machinery and resources necessary for their jobs and their lives. Their unions are company unions in reference to the state and the Communist Party, which absolutely control them. The vital fact in both Russia and Germany is that the function of an owning class under private capitalism has been taken over by a state which itself is a dictatorship without any democratic control. In Russia the process of state control has gone farther than in Germany, and the old capitalist class has been completely and ruthlessly liquidated. The German method of controlling by cajolery and coercion the owning class and its technicians has worked better in terms of orderly production. Nevertheless, state capitalism in Russia as well as in Germany would seem to be a better name for the economic order than socialism. Perhaps we should invent a new name for it. Both in Russia and Germany, despite the different degrees of state ownership, the spread between the income of the rich, or the bureaucrats, and the poor is enormous.

In foreign policy, until Stalin made the deal with Hitler which made possible the beginning of the Second World War, his record was better. He had abstained from national aggression in Europe. Nevertheless the quality of his support of Communist movements in other lands had given some indication of an imperialist attitude. During the "united front" period his help to the Loyalists of Spain, which proved inadequate, was given at a great price, not only in gold but in the kind of control which he tried to set up over the Spanish government and people. But in fairness one must add that it was not Stalin, but Hitler—and to a less extent Mussolini—who menaced the peace of Europe before 1939. Then in the summer of 1939, Stalin helped to unleash the monster, war, by a deal with Hitler in which he doubtless sought his own ends, not Hitler's. But that partnership would have been impossible, had not the inexorable inner logic of the totalitarian form of organization knit the fascist and communist states, despite their hostile origin, into a common pattern of life, thought, and Machiavellianism in government.

To me, the saddest aspect of the whole world-wide tragedy is to be found in the betrayal of the hopes of mankind by the Russian revolution. I never was a communist. I was always hostile to the great Lenin's obvious acceptance of the dogma that "the end justifies the means." I early agreed with Rosa Luxemburg that his "dictatorship of the proletariat" might become a "dictatorship over the proletariat." I always doubted whether with the abolition of private capitalism and the liquidation of a capitalist class, dictatorship and the state itself would wither away. For men covet power as much as property. Nevertheless, for many years I hoped, at first with confidence, that in the midst of thunder and clouds and darkness we had seen over Russia the red dawn of a new and glorious day. Not all at once, but gradually, unwillingly, I have come to substantial agreement with the position taken by Freda Utley in her poignant book *The Dream We Lost*. Perhaps in Miss Utley's Russia, as in Rauschning's Germany, "things can't be quite that bad"; and I want no war between Germany and Russia. But it is conservative to say on the record that Stalin's rule is as cruel and ruthless, as far from true democracy or true socialism, as Hitler's own. The processes of its humanization will be as slow, or slower. If the sacred books of socialism, which Stalin still preserves, are far nobler than Hitler's, the hypocrisy of the actuality is so much the greater. It is the degradation of socialism in Russia that is largely responsible for the disillusionment and confusion of the working class. It is because the dream of socialism in Russia—even Lenin's type of socialism—was lost that the rise of fascism to such great power was possible. This meant that a fearful share of guilt for the Second World War would lie on Stalin's head, even if he had not added to it by those agreements with Hitler which made it possible for the latter safely to begin his war of aggression.

Nevertheless the Second World War in its basic origins was the renewal of an old imperialist conflict in disorganized Europe, not primarily to be attributed to Stalin's machinations on one hand, or to Anglo-French love of democracy on the other. William Henry Chamberlin in a recent magazine article suggests that the older imperialism or the democracies, including America, were unable to save European civilization from the "internal cycle of war and revolution" for lack of a sense of purpose and direction. He writes (*Harper's* December 1940): "The most unfailing characteristic of a régime that is in danger of revolutionary overthrow is not hard-boiled brutality, but a kind of perplexed softness, the fruit of a lack of inner confidence." His remarks are illuminating, but it must be remembered that the "perplexed softness" of the British and French governments was at all times self-interested. They wanted peace, but not at the price of any loss of power, prestige or profit, or any serious modification of their old familiar ways of empire.

It is absurd to join the now popular chorus that the outstanding crime of the Anglo-French Allies was appeasement. The Allies never practised a consistent and well conceived program of appeasement of Germany. What they, more especially Britain, sought to do was to turn Hitler against Russia, or at the last moment appease him at the expense of the Czechs. It was not a noble act, but it had the overwhelming support of the peoples of England and France. Certainly both countries were even less well prepared for war in August

1938 than in August 1939, and the alternative to "appeasement" at the last moment would almost certainly have been war. The crime was not Munich so much as the long series of blunders or worse of which Munich was the natural consequence.

It is equally absurd to argue that if the British had not been so suspicious of Stalin, and if the isolationists had not been so strong in America, a collective security of the British and French Empires, Stalin's Russia, and the United States of America could have been arrived at, and that this would have checked Hitler, perhaps without war. The great lesson of the years is the fact that a negative collective security of that sort was impossible under the dominant loyalties of nationalism and capitalism. No set of international alliances would have given the French the morale which they possessed in the exhausting years of the First World War. That had been undermined partly by the weariness the First World War left behind, partly by political corruption, the economic dominance of the 200 families, the stupidity of the generals, and a lack of confidence in the strength of democracy or its ability to bring security. Economic and military alliance with the United States would not have changed this condition. We had not enough of wisdom and resolution to give; we were not prepared for foreign wars and Hitler knew it. It is certain that if the United States had entered the war on September 1, it would have been unable seriously to change the result for France. We should simply have shared British and French mistakes.

Russia, indeed, might have changed the picture in the military sense. Hitler did not think it wise to begin his aggression against Poland until he had made sure of an understanding with Stalin, but it is questionable whether a wiser diplomacy than the Chamberlain government ever displayed could have made a trustworthy ally out of Stalin. The latter had exacted from Spanish friends a terrible price for his aid. There is more than Krivitsky's word to make one doubt how he would have fulfilled his pledges to France at the time of the Munich crisis, and it seems clear that in the summer of 1939 he wanted from the British and French the free hand in the Baltic states and possibly eastern Poland which Hitler later let him take.

At last the time came when the British and French governments had to fight or surrender their hegemony of Europe and parts of their own empires to Hitler without a struggle. They promised Poland military support against Hitler's demands, although Poland's case was worse rather than better than Czechoslovakia's. The British people, though not the French people, were more intent upon war than their government, yet the war which the Allies declared when Poland was attacked was half-heartedly and inefficiently waged. Statesmen, generals, and admirals displayed an incredible over-confidence. They learned nothing from the destruction of Poland, which they had been powerless to hinder in the slightest degree. The preparation of expeditionary forces in Great Britain went very slowly; the all-important air armament was pushed slowly; it was not until May 1940 that the English worked their war factories on Sundays.

The diplomatic offensive of the Allies was as inept as the military. They had no peace plans to propose to the Europe of 1940, except the old plan of 1914; that is, to defeat the wicked Germans, and all would be well.

After the dreadful débâcle of the blitzkrieg and the fall of France, the British people rallied magnificently. It almost seemed as if they were intent on proving, once more, that the English lose every battle except the last. And in certain respects this last battle is a battle of civilians more than of the military. The jest "join the army and escape the War" has had its point in the London of nightly bombings whose heroes are the organized civilians who work by day and fight fire and disaster by night and keep their courage high. Great Britain's rally was accompanied by new purpose and new organization at home. The Churchill government is genuinely a national government in which the Labor Party has an increasing degree of power. Although all the constitutional guaranties won since ancient times are suspended in the war, the British in fighting for their lives have shown a regard for civil liberty, and an understanding and tolerance of the position of conscientious objectors, which cannot be too highly praised. At home in England there was developing toward the end of 1940, a spirit which offered hope—not certainty— that the inevitable revolution will be toward a democratic socialism rather than fascism or any totalitarianism. The old social order has gone, the old class lines are go-

49

ing; a free and independent democratic England may yet pioneer in a new democracy, as more than a hundred years ago she pioneered in the old.

Yet even this hope must be qualified. There has not emerged a British policy for the reorganization of Europe, or for the substitution of something more adequate to the world peace than the old imperialism. Not even the presence of Labor men in the cabinet has meant an assured promise of independence to India, or has kept the British from imprisoning Nehru, one of the greatest and most idealistic of the Indian people, because he preached a passive resistance to a war that certainly is not India's.

It was not only the British government which at the beginning of 1941 had not stated its war aims, or peace terms. It was the British Labor Party also. Neither in its record nor in the personality of its leaders, even of its strongest man, Ernest Bevin, has there been the assurance one could wish for a new and adequate program for the empire (as distinct from Britain herself) or Europe. As late as the spring of 1937, Mr. Bevin was vehemently trying to justify to me the hypocritical non-intervention policy of the Baldwin government in Spain, and he was much irritated by my interest in the Indian problem. War and responsibility may be educating him. Of his strength, ability and general loyalty to the English workers I have no doubt.

But I have the gravest of fears on two questions: First, the effect of an American alliance on the rise of democratic socialism in England. I suspect that even the

Roosevelt Administration will find itself instinctively more sympathetic with that orator, gentleman, and leader, Winston Churchill, who is nevertheless imperialist to the core of his being, than with Mr. Bevin. Certainly, dominant elements in America will be. For public sentiment, I repeat, especially in powerful financial circles, looks, mistakenly but earnestly, on the salvation of the British Empire as equivalent to the salvation of the social order which our middle and upper classes still cherish. Moreover they want such profits as may—they hope—be salvaged out of cooperation with the empire in its future rule. If—or when—America gets into this war, those of us who believe that whatever hope there may be lies in the growing strength of British socialism have our work cut out for us.

My second fear is more fundamental and far-reaching. Suppose Britain with or without Mr. Roosevelt's help finds the formula for reorganizing Europe which she has not found; suppose that with or without American troops she can reconquer the European continent— which is extraordinarily dubious; what sort of human material will survive the war on either side the Channel to build the new world? This war may become more and more like the Thirty Years War in its confusion and suffering and indefinite duration. Mr. Churchill himself speaks in terms of two or three more years of war. With us all the way in, it will almost certainly be fought on two oceans and five continents. In any event it will be fought by competitive starvation endured by civilian populations who must try to live their lives under the horror of almost nightly raids from the air and the destruction of bombings which do not spare the homes of men or the noblest monuments of Europe's common civilization. Medical skill and good fortune cannot forever stave off the epidemics which have always accompanied great wars. What will be left for building the future? What sort of new generation, starved in body and sick in soul with the horrors amid which they have grown up, will be left for the tasks that lie ahead? What formula of democracy can they carry out? Granting that the peoples of occupied countries will hate Germany and the Germans, will they love England and the English after two, three, four, or more years of blockade? Or will new hates be added to the old?

Man has learned something about the strength of materials. No urgent need or moral necessity, he knows, will enable him to subject a pine plank to the strain that only a steel girder can bear. But of his own nature he knows—and wants to know—far less. Because under the exaltation of war for their homes, the people of London's slums, about the worst in the world, have written such glorious pages in history, our intellectuals assume, against all reason and common sense, that years of this sort of war will condition men, women, and children, not for near insanity, but for democracy and peace! Alas, that cannot be. The thoughtful English writer, John Middleton Murry, has warned his people that the war is conditioning the masses to the temperament which will endure and use violence, not alone against a foreign foe but for unreflective social revolution. He makes an even surer point (*Peace News*, December 6, 1940) concerning the relations of war socialization to peace socialization. The former, he believes, is "the diabolical antithesis of the latter, and war socialization cannot be changed to peace socialization except by an effort of imagination on a grand scale to which the war mentality itself is the chief obstacle." One who remembers the terribly retrogressive elements in the revolutions which followed the First World War will heed Mr. Murry's words.

As I write there seems to be no possibility of a negotiated peace. But such a possibility may emerge sooner than we think. To prepare for it, to get the world thinking about war aims, to create a situation in which even the German people may come to see their dictator as responsible for continuing war—this is a task worth while, not to be damned by calling it appeasement. A peace far from perfect might yet be better than a new Thirty Years War on a worldwide scale. Out of such a war the most probable victor is exhaustion, chaos, and dark night; or perchance, such a breakup of western civilization that that cruel, mediocre, but patient dictator Stalin, with his vast armies and devoted communist followers might pick up the pieces and build his own totalitarianism. Hitler's could hardly be as impervious to any humanizing or liberalizing influence.

Under all these circumstances, to dismiss the very idea of a negotiated peace, simply as "appeasement" or "treason" is a mistake for which the world, and most of all Europe, may pay dear. If it is not our business to tell the English they must stop fighting—and it is not— neither is it our business to tell them they must keep on forever. Our definite conclusions on this subject must, however, await more detailed analysis of America's possible rôle.

CHAPTER IV ☆ AMERICA AND THE WORLD WAR

WHEN Franklin Delano Roosevelt took office March 4, 1933, it was as President of a country tremendously preoccupied with its own economic problems. So far as it had time to think of foreign affairs, the country was predominantly but not intelligently "isolationist." It had got its fingers burned in one European war; it had been unable to collect its debts; investments in Latin America had been almost as unfortunate as, let us say, in Sam Insull's Midwest Holding Company. Dollar diplomacy wasn't paying dividends. Nobody seriously proposed armament economics as a cure for depression, and no sane man saw much reason in great armament. Indeed, there was none until after Hitler had begun the rearmament of Germany—unless the United States entertained very aggressive ambitions in the Far East.

We Americans held highly moral notions on world affairs, except perhaps when those moral notions were likely to cost us something. We objected to other people's imperialism, and we thought in a vague sort of way that international disarmament, or at least limitation of arms, would be a good thing.

Foreign policy was emphatically not Mr. Roosevelt's principal preoccupation in those first months of brilliant achievement. He did, however, find on his doorstep a proposal for an international economic conference in

London. This idea, at first, he blessed. Later, after the conference had actually begun, he became extravagantly afraid of its performance and relentlessly put it to death. Under the conditions of the spring of 1933 any American President would have been ill-advised who put too much confidence in the results of an international economic conference. Nevertheless, even then, such a conference might have made some contribution to the attitude and technique necessary to an economy appropriate to the needs of the world.

Mr. Roosevelt's rapid shift from one extreme to another in dealing with the economic conference is characteristic of his approach to other tremendous issues. Thus, in the summer of 1936, at Chautauqua he delivered an eloquent speech which became the Bible for the isolationists; a little over a year later in Cook County, Illinois—where a Democratic President, contemplating the deeds of his fellow Democrats in the Kelly-Nash machine, might well be excused for talking about China—Mr. Roosevelt in a few unexpected sentences gave to the advocates of collective security words of holy writ by reference to joint action "to quarantine aggressor nations." But his administration never backed either of these conflicting scriptures with appropriate deeds before the outbreak of the war.

In the Far East the President continued the Stimson policy of non-recognition of the puppet government of Manchukuo which Japan had set up by force. He also kept American marines in Shanghai and other ports in

China, and American gunboats on the Yang-tse River. The Chinese, who had strenuously objected to their presence in the 'twenties, accepted them after Japan had begun her active aggression, as a possible counterweight to Japanese force. In general, the administration continued the time-honored American policy of demanding an open door for trade in China while supporting a closed door in the Philippines.

Perhaps the most serious of President Roosevelt's contradictions lay in his dealing with Japanese imperialism after the undeclared war on China was begun. The President mixed denunciation of, with aid to, Japanese imperialism with amazing impartiality. The Treasury continued the purchase of Japanese gold, a disguised subsidy to Japan of less than no value to the United States. It was that purchase of gold which in no small measure accounted for Japanese ability to buy the raw materials necessary for her war of aggression. I grant that the President faced a very difficult situation, but an Administration as resourceful as his and as little bound by the letter of the law, could certainly have found ways quietly, at the very beginning, to discontinue the purchase of Japanese gold and greatly to reduce the stream of raw materials from America to Japan. The latter result might have been accomplished by a thoroughgoing policy of neutrality which would not have affected China adversely since China was not in a position in any case to import great quantities of American arms or raw materials for arms. That might have required supplementary legislation, but even the law of 1937 was never applied in the Far East, although Congress clearly had not intended to limit its application to declared warfare.

In European crises prior to the Second World War, when America had to act, Mr. Roosevelt kept close to the British line. I have already commented on this in discussing the sorry Spanish episode. At the very end of that chapter, our administration, following the British lead, promptly recognized General Franco, without even trying to use American recognition as any sort of lever to move him in the direction of a more tolerant attitude toward his defeated enemies. At the time of the Munich crisis, Mr. Roosevelt very promptly threw his influence on the side of peace. He was not directly responsible for the terms of the Munich agreement, but as late as October 25, 1938, in a statement praising Governor Frank Murphy of Michigan for showing patience in the sit-down strikes, he commended "the cool heads" who in the European crisis "pleaded for continuance of negotiations." A day later, however, the President was denouncing "peace by fear" in an address to the Women's Forum, held under the auspices of the *New York Herald Tribune,* and this speech was widely regarded as an attack on the Munich "settlement."

Whether or not there were any commitments, official or unofficial, written or oral, by the administration to the support of Hitler's enemies, it is certain that as early as the spring of 1937 I found the universal expectation in high and low circles in Britain and on the Continent that the President would again come to the rescue of the

European democracies in the event of war. Several months before the actual outbreak of the Second World War the President, in a celebrated interview, in effect assured members of the Senate Foreign Relations Committee that our frontier was on the Rhine. He later denied the use of this phrase; two different Senators on separate occasions have told me the denial was verbally correct, but that the phrase was a weak summary of the ideas that the President then expressed.

During the political campaign of 1940 the Republicans and the Democrats bitterly arraigned each other for the inadequacy of our military establishment. It seems clear that the President had always got about what he asked for, and that prior to the blitzkrieg he had asked for the very considerable sum of more than 7 billion dollars. Referring to the President's message of January 28, 1938, so good an authority as Charles A. Beard observed, "He demanded an enormous increase of naval outlay and a Mobilization Bill which had no meaning unless he wanted a huge army which could be used in Europe." For the weaknesses of our army which he later so loudly deplored, it would appear that the lack of co-ordination so vividly described by Oswald Garrison Villard in his little book *Our Military Chaos* was largely responsible.

The two bright spots of the administration's foreign policy before the war were its Good Neighbor program in Latin American affairs and its support of reciprocal trade agreements. In the first instance President Roosevelt's Secretary of State, Cordell Hull, developed with patience, skill and success, a policy of using conciliation rather than marines in Latin America—a policy which may be said to have begun when President Coolidge sent Dwight Morrow as Ambassador to Mexico. The trade policy was Secretary Hull's own, and if the world had not lost itself in war and war economics, it might have gone much farther than it did toward better economic relationship between peoples.

When the Second World War finally began on September 1, 1939, two facts about American public opinion immediately became apparent: (1) Condemnation of Hitler and sympathy with the Allies were almost universal, but (2) there was a firm determination in the minds of an overwhelming majority of the American people that their country must keep out of war. President Roosevelt clearly shared the first feeling. It is doubtful if he shared the second to an equal degree, but he was quite too shrewd a politician not to recognize it and bow to it. On September 7, 1939, the *New York Times* published a summary of a talk between the President and some unnamed New York friend. This summary was reported as recognizing that the abandonment of the neutrality restrictions which then existed was an extremely delicate subject in view of public opinion, but Mr. Roosevelt thought that various incidents "would quickly bring America's reaction to the boiling point." The conclusion of the matter was this: "Once Congress convened, with the abandonment of neutrality restrictions as the purpose of the session, the chief question was expected to be the degree of participation in war which the American people will tolerate." *

But by the time Congress met to consider the revision of the Neutrality Law, the President sang a different tune. He talked about "international law" and "true neutrality" and American defense in support of the law's revision—arguments which, in the words of Arthur Krock of the *New York Times,* were "insincere and inaccurate and did not disclose his real purposes." He and his followers in the whole debate adopted a strategy of advancing the old isolationist cash-and-carry measure as an alternative to the isolationists' arms embargo and a better proposal for keeping America out of war. Both proposals were originally part of the same program; the conflict between them was fictitious.

It would be presuming too much to judge the President's inner motives or to deny the objective sincerity of his reiterated desire to keep America out of actual belligerent participation in war, but it is not unfair to say that, given American public opinion, a President wishing to put the country all or part way into war would scarcely have adopted a program different from Mr. Roosevelt's. "Isolationists" lost the fight on the Neutrality Bill, but their fight and the indications the American public gave of opposition of entry into war have been a very great factor in keeping us out.

Weeks before the final passage of the revised Neutrality Law, Poland had been conquered. The war, except

* For a fuller discussion of this and for citations see *Keep America Out of War* by Norman Thomas and Bertram D. Wolfe (Stokes).

on the seas, had settled down into what many Americans openly said was a "phony" war or a "sits-krieg." In the winter of 1939–40 it was the Russian attack upon Finland which aroused American indignation and active sympathy for the Finns. The British and French governments did not want American troops, and in both countries there was a considerable sentiment that they did not want American intervention. In the British Parliament, God was asked by a speaker to deliver England from a German victory or an American peace. Allied purchases under the Neutrality Law were decidedly less than many had imagined, anticipated, or hoped. Great Britain deliberately bought all the supplies she could either in her own empire, where it was obviously easy to peg her currency, or in countries like Turkey, whose favor she courted. Military orders, also, were less than was expected. The same issue of the *New York Times* which brought the news of the beginning of the German blitzkrieg on the Low Countries, carried a dispatch from Washington, which recited the fact that although the combined British and French production of airplanes was decidedly lower than before the war, orders by their governments for American airplanes were much smaller than had been anticipated. This, be it remembered, was a month after the daring German attack on Norway, which many military and naval experts still believe should not have succeeded. Some observers are convinced that it was this success that finally turned the scales in Hitler's mind in favor of aggressive war in the west. It took the blitzkrieg itself to make the British start the flood of orders in America.

During this whole period, the winter and early spring of 1940, not only was the pressure for American participation in war greatly lessened, but the expectation of it, as inevitable, was sharply reduced. There was even a considerable interest in the possibility of negotiated peace which was actually favored by the small nations of the old Oslo bloc. The socialists in those countries made no secret of their hope that President Roosevelt would take some initiative in this matter, and he did belatedly make tentative feelers in the direction of peace, including the sending of Sumner Welles, Under Secretary of State, to Europe to spy out the situation.

The fearful success of the blitzkrieg completely changed the picture. The "phony" war had become a desperate reality. France fell, and the very life, not only of the British Empire but of England itself, was at stake. America was confronted with a new and completely unexpected situation. To discuss the origins of the war, the mistakes that had led to it, its imperialist nature—all that had become for the moment academic. What would happen to America and American interests if Hitler should be able to install in London a government as subservient to him as that with which he dealt in France? That was the question.

If the United States had been in any sort of shape to wage aggressive war in Europe speedily, it is possible that the President would have put us in the conflict.

We were in no such shape. The question of our own defense became of primary importance. Our own safety, it was generally believed, would be greatly served by preserving British power, but there was a widespread feeling, even in official circles, that it might already be too late to save Great Britain. Hence the government was forced to strike a rough and changing balance between concentrating on our own defense and sending "all possible" military supplies to Great Britain.

Not long before the blitzkrieg two newspaper men, Messrs. Alsop and Kintner, had written an unofficial *American White Paper* which had the Presidential blessing. It expressed a faith and hope on the part of the administration that the country was adequately prepared to patrol the Far East in our own interests, but more largely in the interests of western imperialism, to police this hemisphere, and to exercise great influence on the side of righteousness in Europe. All this, in the expectation of the President, without sending troops abroad. The book was just gaining headway as a best seller when the President felt compelled to appear before Congress to tell us that most of the armaments which we had acquired prior to the outbreak of the Second World War were obsolete, and to suggest that we could scarcely defend Omaha against German bombers, operating by way of South America, Yucatan, and the Mississippi Valley on a time table a tourist company might follow, given fair weather.

This speech and the President's subsequent words and deeds augmented a near hysteria which he, and he

64

alone, might have abated.* But, on the whole, the President was able to make that hysteria increase, rather than diminish, his political support. He was the horse who ought not to be swapped while we were crossing the stream of crisis; and the public accepted this as true, despite the fact that neither in his historic address to Congress, nor subsequently, did the President ever give clear evidence of forthright facing of two essential questions: First, what should we defend; and second, how should we defend it. Defense in the months following the blitzkrieg was variously defense of our shores, defense of the western hemisphere, defense of our interests, defense of democracy, defense of civilization, defense of Christianity, etc. Our eastern frontier, pushed back from the Rhine became the English Channel; our western frontier was somewhere between Shanghai and Singapore.

If neither the President nor the people was ready to answer explicitly the question "What shall we defend?" it is no wonder that they were even vaguer in answering the second question "How shall we defend it?" There is no evidence that there ever was any proper council of the wisest experts, men who could be found in civilian life and the military service, to examine the lessons of

* The lovers of Great Britain for her own sake and the sincere internationalists who believe that "democracy and liberty are indivisible" and hence want intervention, would be astonished at the immense preponderance of sheer fear in popular support of "aid to Britain" as I have tested it in all parts of the country. Moreover, men who when pressed deny that they really fear direct attack on us, in speeches and radio comment consciously and unconsciously cultivate precisely that fear. It does not build a good morale for saving democracy.

modern warfare; to coordinate the branches of our service, and to end our military chaos. We continued to support forts dating back to old Indian days, whose only value was to protect the profits of local chambers of commerce. This failure contributed to our turn toward thoroughgoing armament economics, instead of toward a reasonable program to satisfy the needs of a nation for security against attack.

The President's first request of Congress for supplemental defense appropriations was for $1,182,000,000. He then was exceedingly desirous that Congress should go home. Congress refused. In the next few months the President came back and back, until the total appropriations and authorizations he had won from Congress aggregated some 15 billion dollars, more than in any year of our participation in the First World War; more than the factory payroll of the most prosperous year in American history.

More surprising, even allowing for the state of national hysteria, than the ease with which the nation accepted armament economics and voted for war preparations billions which it would not have thought of spending in the struggle with poverty, was the ease with which the same nation reversed its historic policy by the adoption of peacetime military conscription. Dr. C. A. Dykstra, the Administrator of the Draft, according to the press, confessed soon after taking office, that six months earlier he would never have believed that conscription would be adopted, and adopted so easily, by the American people. It is questionable whether it would have

66

been so easily adopted under any other leadership than President Roosevelt's. He had so won the confidence of the workers of America by his domestic reforms that they followed his foreign policy as they would no other man's. Although the great labor bodies, almost without exception, adopted resolutions, more or less strongly condemning the immediate adoption of peacetime military conscription, the resolutions were mostly paper declarations, never implemented by impressive meetings or demonstrations in industrial centers, and somewhat vitiated in effect by the report of the Gallup poll that the majority of the workers really favored conscription. Manifestations of popular disapproval of conscription would, at least, have postponed it. The significance both of conscription and of armament economics to America's future is so great that it must be further examined when we consider that future.

Along with armament economics and peacetime conscription, the President's policy was one of increasing emphasis, after the courage of the British people had guaranteed them against immediate collapse, upon "all aid to England short of war." What was short of war, he never openly determined. On the contrary, he committed what would undoubtedly have been acts of war under any ordinary circumstances when he exchanged fifty destroyers in the possession of the American navy, for the permission to use certain strategically placed British possessions in the Western Hemisphere for military and naval bases. The latter permission was valuable; it probably could have been gained, anyhow, on other terms in connection with the joint defense of the United States and Canada.

The President himself had assured the public originally that it was not tied up with the question of destroyers, but in the deal that was consummated the tieup was made, and was made without knowledge or consent of the war-making body, although Congress was in session.

This was the act of a nation which had almost gone to war with Great Britain because of the help she had given, or allowed to be given, to the privateer *Alabama* in Civil War days. It was an act in violation of domestic law, despite the strange interpretation of that law given by the Attorney General. More clearly, it was in violation of the Hague Convention of 1907, which both the United States and Germany had signed. It did not lead to war because war was not to Hitler's interest, but it probably was a factor in finally putting through the treaty between Japan and the Axis powers, which treaty guaranteed that if America should begin war against Japan or Germany, it would have to be fought against both nations on two oceans all around the world.

This gamble of the administration with war met no effective challenge under our two-party system. There was a strong opposition to the administration in Congress which was, on the whole, bi-partisan. In the campaign of 1940 the advocates of armament economics, peacetime military conscription, and "all aid short of war" both to Britain and to China, numbered Wendell Willkie among their adherents as surely as President Roosevelt. The interventionists unquestionably aided Mr. Willkie powerfully, financially and otherwise, in his drive toward nomination, and they used his personal popularity to nullify the comparatively isolationist platform which the Republicans adopted.

It is a commentary on the nature of our democracy and our general political set-up that although the most vital single issue in midsummer of 1940 was peacetime conscription, it was never mentioned in the platform or on the floor of either the Republican or Democratic Nominating Convention. Mr. Roosevelt took occasion to refer to it in accepting his third term nomination, linking, in effect, the conscription of the youth of America, with his own draft for a third term.

Conscription, armament economics, and the limits of aid to Britain were at no time seriously discussed by the major parties in the campaign, although these were the policies which would affect the very lives and destinies of millions of Americans. The campaign ended in a kind of rivalry between the major candidates in personal promises not to send American troops abroad.

Mr. Willkie's one chance of defeating the President was to find an issue with the emotional appeal which the President offered the masses by reason of their identification of economic security with his person and program. Possibly he might have won by giving articulate expression and leadership to the very strong American feeling against involvement in war. His own convictions, perhaps his commitments to powerful backers, made this impossible and he confined himself to unimpressive criticisms of the President on minor points of foreign affairs. Even so, American interest in peace compelled Mr. Roosevelt to stress his own zeal in that cause. He gave no hint that he would demand the dictatorial powers over peace and war which he immediately sought from the new Congress. Whatever excuse there may be for this sort of thing, it paves the way for fascism, not intelligent democracy.

As the President began his third term with an eloquent tribute to democracy in his inaugural address, American relations to the war stood about as follows:

So far had we departed from neutrality that by ordinary precedent, and if this had been the traditional sort of war, we should have been openly in it. As it was, we were non-belligerent. Public opinion was still overwhelmingly against belligerency. But, under the President's leadership and with the propaganda of interventionists well entrenched in press and radio, the majority was not only already committed to aid to Britain but was, if the Gallup poll is correct, increasingly willing to take a chance on aid leading to war. My own contacts made me certain, however, that there was still among millions of the people the belief, nurtured by the President's own statements, either that we should escape belligerency and save the world with *things* and not with *men*, or that belligerency would be partial; that we should send no troops abroad. The overwhelming probability that the complete military victory over Germany and Japan would require all the troops we could raise; that it could mean war in the Pacific as well as the Atlantic, in Asia,

Africa and the islands of the sea as well as Europe, was played down by interventionists. Their supporters in forums and elsewhere were usually irritated by the suggestion that the European continent—to say nothing of Asia—could not be reconquered without troops, and in view of the difficulty of invasion and the strength of German arms, probably not with them; that the war might well be of indefinite duration, with exhaustion or Stalin the only victor.

As I write it seems possible but doubtful that anti-Axis superiority in the air if established, combined with the blockade, might break German morale. But if Germany's great superiority in the air could not reduce England to surrender, ere this, I question whether any probable superiority of British air power will of itself defeat Germany. Britain may, indeed, have valuable help from the occupied nations but it is doubtful if they can arm themselves, or be armed for modern warfare against their masters. The German army will be the last to starve, especially with Russia still a quasi-ally, and it is possible that after months or years of hunger the peoples of western Europe may hate Britain and the blockade almost as much as they hate Hitler. It is our business to face these relative probabilities and possibilities, not ignore them.

Our failure to face reality bodes no good for American morale in a war so different from the expectation of the masses. It may be smart tactics to sidle into total war; it is not an intelligent strategy for seeing that war through.

Short of war, our aid to Britain has been great but

scarcely decisive. We have guaranteed the safety of Canada against attack; we have patrolled the Far East with our navy on behalf of Britain's imperial interests, which are far greater than our own. We changed our laws during the war to permit her to use our productive apparatus to provide all the supplies she could transport. We have even helped her pay for them by the disguised subsidy of our gold purchases to the tune of hundreds of millions of dollars annually. All this was explained to the American people as in our own interest, valuable, if not essential, to our defense.

No one under the circumstances proposed to abate this aid or suddenly to impose such an embargo as the President had clapped on Loyalist Spain. For ten years I had been advocating as the principle which should animate our foreign policy: "the maximum possible co-operation for peace; the maximum possible isolation from war." If that policy had been consistently followed, and we had taken advantage of the relative security we might have established to make our own democracy work, I still think that America and the world would have been better off. But we did not follow that policy. When the war turned from probable stalemate to the Nazi conquest of western Europe and the defense of England against invasion, it would have been monstrous suddenly to restore the partial embargo Congress had repealed. No significant group advocated such a thing, or even complained at giving England priority on the output of our airplane factories and shipyards, and most Americans were open minded on further practicable aid to an England still fighting off the invader.

But many of us were very critical of the President's policy: (1) because it put aid to Britain ahead of keeping out of war, which we felt was our primary duty; (2) it did not even ask Mr. Churchill for his war aims; (3) it was either intended to put us all the way into war crabwise or else it was a mean-spirited exhortation to the British: "Fight on and on and on and we'll sell you, or lend you, or maybe even give you some supplies."

Especially were we appalled at the President's Lend-Lease Bill. As introduced by his order, it was a virtual declaration of war in the name of peace; a breath-taking gamble on American security in the name of defense; and the establishment of dictatorship in the matters most vitally affecting the American people in the name of democracy. Six years—or six months—ago no American would have argued otherwise concerning a bill to permit the President to commit any conceivable act of war except the dispatch of great armies abroad. This grant then had no time limit. Yet this bill of itself did not increase production of ships or planes, nor did it definitely expand British purchasing power. In Congressional hearings cabinet members and other high officials argued for it not on the merits of the bill, but in terms of the old fear motif. A triumphant Hitler, it was suggested rather than openly stated, might conquer this hemisphere by his propaganda and his spies, certainly by his military strength.

Although England, with almost absolute command of

73

the sea, could not successfully reoccupy friendly Norway against a comparative handful of Germans, we are continually asked to believe that Germany can successfully invade this continent, or at any rate this hemisphere. Where are the ports of landing, where enough men or supplies? What would be happening to our own defense program? I have never seen contradicted the oft-quoted statement that a successful invasion of the United States would require at least 1,000,000 troops who, in turn, would need the services of 8,000,000 to 13,000,000 tons of commercial shipping, plus a navy big enough to defeat ours in our waters, and pulverize our coast defenses. It would be easier to make a landing in Brazil, but Brazil's ports are farther from us than Europe; and the walking is poor, and so are the roads. No man or superman could unite sullen slaves in a half-starved Europe successfully to support such a venture against us, unless in our own hysteria we had lost our own morale and our own faith in our own democracy.

To this statement let me add that up until now really effective use of bombers has required bases comparatively near the point of attack. The R.A.F. which has saved England has been relatively ineffective in attacks on Berlin for that reason. Each bomber requires twenty to thirty ground men and elaborately equipped bases, not to be established overnight in South America.

Even worse as a confession of defeat was fear that our democracy could not protect itself by its own inherent strength of morale and the resources of a continent, or, indeed, if we are wise, a friendly and cooperative hemisphere. That is to lose the struggle in advance.

I write while the President's bill is before Congress. I hope that it will at least be drastically amended.*

In a dangerous world, to choose war now is the most dangerous of policies. It is a choice that will make our own totalitarianism sure without a compensating blessing to mankind. The reason for this solemn warning will be more apparent after we have examined our drift to fascism.

Meanwhile America and the world await tensely the rumored all-out attack on Britain by the Nazis, an attack whose decisive failure might pave the way to a more

* After this paragraph was in type the Lend-Lease Bill, somewhat improved by amendments, became law. The President at once dispatched an unrevealed amount and kind of "defense articles" to England, and asked Congress to appropriate seven billion dollars for further aid. By precedent and logic this means war, but the peculiar circumstances of this conflict still make it possible that we shall not be involved to the extent of belligerent use of our own soldiers, sailors, and airmen. But with enactment of this law most of the power of effective decision on this vital point has passed out of the hands not only of Congress and the people, but even of the President to whom such dictatorial powers have been entrusted. Our fate rests largely with Hitler and the Japanese, and the crisis may come soon or late. Even more, perhaps, it rests with Winston Churchill, for, if our main duty is at all costs to aid Britain who is so good a judge of what that duty requires as the brilliant Prime Minister of King George's realm? Altogether it is a desperate gamble which the President has undertaken.

Nevertheless, I think it worth while to keep up the struggle against belligerent participation in war. We should capitalize the strong feeling, repeatedly expressed in the Congressional debate, that in some strange way this law is designed to keep us out of war. The best way I can see to capitalize that feeling in the country, and to put pressure on Congress and the President, is to demand that Congress promise to consult the people by an advisory referendum before it will sanction our full entrance into the war. I am advocating that demand with the full knowleddge of its limitations. In spite of them, it is I think a democratic and relatively practicable proposal.

75

desirable peace than now seems probable and whose success would make American aid by arms too late—unless, indeed, we should be left to carry on alone a war into which we had been recklessly thrust.

CHAPTER V ☆ AMERICA DRIFTS

ANY program of action which concerns itself with reality must be in the realm of the possible. It cannot be a mere exercise of the imagination in constructing a desirable Utopia. It is not necessary, however, to prove that a *possible* program of action must be *probable* or to argue that that for which men should work will in any case be the probable result of existing tendencies or social forces—in short, that we shall drift to a desirable society.

Quite the contrary is the case. America, shouting the praises of democracy, drifts to her own brand of fascism. It is an oft-told tale that the late Huey Long was once asked whether America could go fascist and replied, "Sure, but we'll call it anti-fascist."

This fear of an American fascism was formulated in my mind early in the great depression. I referred to it frequently in the campaign of 1932 and it inspired a book which I published in 1933 entitled *The Choice Before Us*. I based my fear on now familiar grounds: the failure of our economic order to provide jobs, and the failure of regular governmental agencies or institutions to meet the crisis or to inspire confidence. A fascist attempt to deal with these failures seemed to me the more likely because fascist methods and tactics were congenial to a country so familiar with, and tolerant of, gangsterism, lynching, racial feeling and those multifarious organizations which, in the 'thirties, were crowd-

77

ing into the place filled by the Ku Klux Klan in the 'twenties.

This drift to fascism was definitely arrested by President Roosevelt and his New Deal. He did make some regular provision for the unemployed. He showed real sympathy for the underdog. He awakened hope and gave to the masses new confidence in the regular, duly constituted government.

By these processes the growth of an American fascism was arrested; not prevented. Many of Mr. Roosevelt's administrative devices could be taken over by a fascist, as well as by a democratic state. Then it could be argued that they had prepared the way for such a state. Americans, however, have reason to be devoutly thankful not only that Mr. Roosevelt was not, and is not, by desire or intention, a fascist, but also that he has used his oratorical power and his popularity with the masses consciously to extol democracy. Nevertheless, even if war had not again convulsed the world, the failure of the New Deal to make a reformed capitalism, under democratic auspices, work for the removal of insecurity and unemployment left the taproot of fascism unimpaired. What Mr. Roosevelt did was largely the result of a personal leadership insufficiently reflected in the reorganization of government, or in the spirit of his own political party.

And democracy, as contrasted with fascism, while it cannot dispense with leadership, desperately needs to develop organized forms of action superior to those which it inherited from the nineteenth and early twentieth centuries. Neither the labor movement nor our organized political parties adequately meet the needs of democracies in crisis. The campaign of 1940 was discouraging to anyone who hoped that American democracy was developing those attitudes and techniques of rational discussion of grave issues which the crisis demanded. Simply on the basis of the political and economic situation as depicted, for instance, in as conservative a magazine as *Fortune* for February 1940, from which I have already quoted, we should have had reason to struggle against the drift to fascism—a fascism springing more probably from developments of our present constitutional government than from conquest of it by any shirted organization.

But it was the new World War, more specifically, the success of the German attack on Norway, the Low Countries and France, which tightened and made more immediate the danger of our own fascism. One can almost date it from the blitzkrieg.

This danger does not spring as yet from conscious imitation of Germany, or from the success of German propaganda or German intrigue. The latter seems to me surprisingly unsuccessful. At the beginning of 1941, despite all our talk about "fifth columns" and "Trojan horses," there was little evidence of their activity in public opinion, as expressed at the election, or in the Gallup and similar polls. Neither has a presumably competent FBI turned up much evidence of the activities of spies and saboteurs. It was our own fear which had made us turn toward our own fascism as a protection against foreign fascism, toward our own modified Hitlerism as a rampart against Hitler.

The state of civil liberties is a vital test of the drift toward fascism. From the spring of 1937 until about the time of the blitzkrieg we Americans could take great comfort to ourselves that our civil liberties were better protected by law and by custom than at any time perhaps in our national history. The protection was far from perfect—no federal anti-lynching law had been enacted, racial discrimination, industrial espionage, various forms of organized gangsterism and intolerance, were still writing black pages in our history. Yet our skies were bright with hope.

Then came the hysteria which the blitzkrieg provoked, and soon thereafter, perhaps by coincidence, the retrogressive decision of the Supreme Court in the case of the Witnesses for Jehovah; then, not by coincidence, an outburst of mob violence against these sectarians; and also not by coincidence, the passage of the drastic Smith Alien and Sedition Law.

The Witnesses for Jehovah are sincere, persistent, almost fanatical sectarians, very intolerant of other sects and churches, particularly of the Roman Catholic. Their methods of propaganda by systematic tract selling, with the aid of phonographs, does not endear them to the public. Yet they have been guilty of no overt acts whatsoever against the government or the orderly life of our communities. If freedom of religion has meaning, it has meaning for them.

They came into conflict with the law wholly because

they believe that to salute the flag is a form of idolatry, and many states by law require such a salute in the public schools. We then had the spectacle of whole communities, for instance in Boss Hague's New Jersey, in the midst of war, depression, and political corruption, being shaken by the subversive import of little Johnny Jones's refusal to perform what his father had told him was an idolatrous act.

The Witnesses for Jehovah claimed that they were protected in their refusal to salute the flag by the Constitutional guaranty of freedom of religion. At last the issue came before the Supreme Court of the United States, which, in an eight-to-one decision written, under one of history's ironies, by that former crusader for civil liberty, Felix Frankfurter, held that if and when legislative bodies enact laws requiring certain acts as part of a patriotic ritual ministering to the unity of the state, their judgment must be final.

It is a decision which Hitler might have applauded. Why else does he keep Pastor Niemoeller amidst the horrors of a concentration camp? The Nazi rulers never ordered that Christian pastor to bow the knee to Baal, or to worship any of the gods of the Wagnerian operas. His quarrel with them simply concerned the question of what his church owed to the state by way of patriotic obedience. Our Supreme Court, by rather similar methods of reasoning, has laid the foundation of a religion of the state in America at a time when the religion of the state is the chief bulwark of totalitarianism.

The Supreme Court decision was a lighted match to a

powder flame of sadistic mob patriotism. In at least forty-four states, before the summer was over, Witnesses for Jehovah had suffered severely in person and property. Most of these crimes were not considered worth reporting by the press, except perhaps in the districts where they occurred. There were over 335 instances of mob violence involving 1,488 men, women and children; some of them, as I discovered in the course of my travels, were monstrously brutal.

By the end of June 1940 Congress had enacted, and the President had signed, the Smith Alien and Sedition Law, almost without notice by the country, except for that section of the law which required the registration and fingerprinting of aliens—this, on the theory that from those fingerprints the government can distinguish the foot marks of the Trojan horses which threaten our land. I was no enthusiast for this type of legislation lest it minister to regimentation, but it does not disturb me greatly.

The really dangerous feature of the bill went almost unprotested even by lovers of civil liberty. It is the clause which under the guise of preventing disaffection in the military forces of the United States can be used in peace-time for more drastic restrictions on the discussion of foreign policy than was possible under the Espionage Act in the First World War. It is fair to say that up to the present time the law has not been thus used by the Roosevelt Administration, but its significance in the hands of a reactionary or hysterical prosecutor is thoroughly fascist.

That same summer, except for a mixture of good fortune and the parliamentary skill of Senator Danaher of Connecticut, whose amendments made the legislation relatively innocuous, Congress would have passed a bill, born of legitimate desire to set up control over parties owing allegiance to foreign rulers, which would have imposed impossible conditions on political parties, labor unions, and other groups which had international affiliations. The bill, one of the fruits of the Dies Committee's technique, voiced a more intolerant nationalism than was dreamed of in the First World War. That type of intolerant nationalism is a natural ally of fascism.

In general, during the whole campaign of 1940, an understandable mistrust of the Communist Party resulted in steps to put it off the ballot, but these steps went clear beyond the bounds of democratic procedure. Opposition to Communists also influenced public officials in many states to interpret and enforce already stringent election laws so that in a larger number of states than ever before it was difficult to the point of impossibility for a minority party to get on the ballot. The tendency to have a two-party monopoly of the ballot (and logically if only two, why not only one?) was sharply increased. But the really revolutionary change in the American way of life, clearly in the direction of totalitarianism, was the adoption of peacetime military conscription. It is nominally for a five-year period, but it is already evident that in some form it will almost certainly be made permanent, more or less regardless of the issue of the present war, unless Americans can be aroused to straighter thinking about it than they have heretofore shown.

Sincere men and women who support conscription will challenge this statement. They will say that conscription was necessary to meet a grave national peril; that it was the most democratic of ways to meet that peril. They may add that it has positive advantages for morale and health. Well, let us see.

In whatever military sense conscription might be considered necessary, it was not for the purpose of the defense of our shores. That task the army has no intention of entrusting primarily to one-year conscripts, but to the professional soldiers who form the core of the air force, the coast artillery, and the mechanized units. Such defense will be the duty of the navy, to which conscription has not yet been applied. Conscription is necessary in a military sense only if great expeditionary forces are contemplated. That such was the case was proved by the administration's insistence that the President should be given the right to send the conscript troops anywhere he might choose, at least in this hemisphere. When I appeared before the Senate Military Affairs Committee in opposition to conscription, Senator Minton of Indiana, then the Democratic whip and a chief spokesman for the administration, questioned me solely along lines of the necessity for conscription to enable the government to face a situation in which Brazil might have a government hostile to us. At all events, the administration won the right to send our boys much farther from home than western Europe without the necessity of any formal declaration of war, and it was argued with some force in Congress that once the right was granted to the Commander in Chief of the army to send conscript troops beyond our borders, his discretion could not be confined to this hemisphere. However that may be, Congress granted by this law to the President a virtual war power which by any correct use of words is dictatorial. It did it in a time of hysteria. It did it at a time when not only some employers but many workers openly welcomed conscription for the army as a new kind of WPA, as a way to end unemployment.

At no time was such a moderate argument against the necessity for conscription as was advanced by Hanson W. Baldwin, military expert of the *New York Times*, in *Harper's Magazine* for August 1940, answered in any detail. Fear swept us. It was only after the bill was safely passed that Col. Frederick Palmer smugly admitted in his syndicated articles (for instance *New York Times*, October 6, 1940) that it was no longer necessary to appeal to "the false scare of land invasion" to get adequate military preparedness in America.

But, some men argued, even if conscription was not absolutely necessary to raise an army for defense, it was the most democratic way to get it—more democratic than voluntary enlistment which at the time conscription was adopted was easily filling the quota sought, in spite of the fact that the minimum term of enlistment was kept at three years, and no effort had been made to offer such attractive conditions as those which later were offered to conscripts. Here again, one must observe that it is a Nazi rather than a liberal concept of democracy which is satisfied by the equality of a peacetime conscription which our fathers regarded as slavery to the state.

In America it is hardly a concept of equality, since luck and the draft boards have so much to do with the selection of men. At the worst, conscription might easily be used as a powerful weapon to beat down labor agitation. All that is necessary is to refuse to a young "agitator" the affidavit of necessity for work in some airplane factory, easily granted to his associates in like case. The draft boards will do the rest. Already in California the first effort—repudiated by the central administration—has been made to use the draft to break a strike. If the selective draft is the ideal principle of democracy in filling useful and necessary callings, why should it not be extended to the police, fire, and street-cleaning departments? One could easily make a case that there are lounge lizards who could be better employed sweeping streets, on which tasks "mute, inglorious Miltons" may now be wasting their talents.

I still believe that one of the most valuable of civil liberties is the right of a man to determine how his own life should be invested, and that if he is to give this right up at all, even for one year, it would be better on terms approaching William James's celebrated moral equivalent for war, rather than for preparation for war.

The arguments for military camps to build body and mind have little validity. They would have no validity at all, except for disgraceful failure in the matter of housing, employment and proper health education. The discipline of the army is not, and cannot be made, the discipline of democracy. The life of an army camp cannot be made completely normal. No father who could help it would dream of living on the edge of an army camp with young daughters. One of the most disquieting things about our adoption of conscription was the number of liberals, especially on college faculties, and in high schools, who seemed to welcome the drill sergeant as an ally in producing that morale which they had not produced through the old American plan of education. Their arguments at this point were confessions of their own failure.

At that, they completely overlooked the inescapable fact that military conscription was the foundation principle of the totalitarian state; that it would be incredible that any people would accept the extreme of dictatorial power over them except that first they had been persuaded to accept it in the name of national security. It is, of course, true that democracies have used conscription, but so far was conscription from automatically saving the morale of France and the Low Countries, that it was the armies which collapsed. It was in the armies in all the occupied countries that the fifth columnists seemed to have been most successfully active.

These and other arguments against conscription were in vain. Congress adopted it by a margin determined by the almost solid support of the South, the least democratic section of the country, for this bill. It adopted it with more generous provisions for conscientious objectors than in the First World War, but less generous provisions than England allowed in the midst of war for her life. The administration went to work to enforce conscription under conditions which would make the sugar coating on the pill as thick as possible. But even fascist dictators can be benevolent to docile subjects.

With less opposition than was directed against military peacetime conscription, Congress and the country went all out for armament economics, that is for gearing our whole economic machinery to the production of arms, first for ourselves and secondarily for Great Britain. The test of armament economics is not merely the size of the appropriations; it is the proportion of them and the central place they hold in the national economy. But the size is important.

To just what we are committed is not clear. The first government department to make a long-range estimate was, curiously enough, the Department of Agriculture, whose economists, according to the *New York Times*, December 6, 1940, reckoned that our program would cost 35 billion dollars in the next five years. The President's 1941 budget message, in tone as well as in figures, made that estimate appear far too low; so did the fact that the navy immediately began demanding more. All this excludes the billions of dollars that aid to England will cost.* Only for defense requirements, and for that

* After this paragraph was in type, Arthur Krock, writing in the *New York Times*, March 12, 1941, reported that "exclusive of the initial costs of the lease-lend policy, appropriations made, authorized or recommended amount to $32 billions for the fiscal years 1940–1941 and 1941–1942." Of this huge sum it is estimated that within those fiscal years a total of $17,275 millions will be spent, leaving $14,725 millions to be spent in subsequent years. On the same day that Mr.

belatedly and imperfectly, was a large element of plan introduced. There had not been an equivalent plan for war against poverty during all the bitter years since 1929. We have had a more exact knowledge of what we needed by way of homes and clothes and food and other consumers' goods in order to be a healthy, happy nation, than we have now of what we need for military security. Yet to fight poverty nobody would have dreamed of appropriating money as we are now appropriating it for military defense.

Unequestionably those appropriations will relieve unemployment. The winter holidays of 1940 were, except for the dark shadow of war, the happiest for twelve long years. There were more jobs and more hopes of jobs; more money to spend for human wants and needs and a greater sense of security. Even war isn't so horrible when it brings these things. The spokesman for airplane workers in California who proposed the gift of a bomber for the British R.A.F. had a realistic approach to the problem. He didn't talk about saving democracy, or even the United States, in Europe. He said, according to the *New York Times* of December 11, 1940, "The British are responsible for many of us working, and we think a Christmas gift would be a fine thing."

Even so, it was a lopsided prosperity that seemed to

Krock made this report the President asked for seven billion dollars more as the beginning of aid to other countries under the Lease-Lend Law. This means a scale of expenditure, even if we escape belligerent participation in this war, far in excess of the estimate quoted from the economists of the Department of Agriculture. We are committed to armament economics with a vengeance.

be returning. The same issue of a daily paper which gave the estimate of the American Federation of Labor that in November 1940 there were 8,135,000 jobless had another estimate from the American Society of Mechanical Engineers that at least one million more skilled employees in the heavy industries would soon be urgently needed. Some weeks later reports from Great Britain told us that in the midst of the war for her life, she still had more than 700,000 unemployed. Armament economics is not a satisfactory answer to the problem of unemployment.

It is no answer at all to the problem of abundance. Imagine the most futile economic enterprise on a great scale which the mind of man can conceive. Let a nation enter upon it enthusiastically enough, and it would provide jobs, and create gigantic vested interests in its continuance, but it would be mad folly. In a purely economic sense armament production—however necessary it may seem in a cruel and predatory world—is the most wasteful of enterprises. Virgil Jordan, President of the National Industrial Conference Board, puts the matter well:

"During the next few years it is probable that from a third to a half of the working capacity, savings, and income of the population will be consumed in this way, and a very high level of business and industrial activity will be maintained by this process so long as it is continued. The country will become more and more insolvent as a result.

"This insolvency will be reflected in an enormous

mass of facilities for production of war equipment, the rapid depreciation and destruction of facilities for producing the ordinary economic requirements of the population, the cessation of investment in such facilities, and the diversion to war occupations of a large and increasing part of the working population from employment in producing the things they need to live on. It will result in a steady and rapid decline in the standard of living, and, when the process stops, in the most profound and prolonged depression which this country or the world has ever experienced, in the course of which most business enterprises will be bankrupted, the value of all individual savings and life insurance will be reduced or wiped out and all public debts repudiated." (Quoted from the *Call,* January 4, 1941.)

Obviously, armament economics must be paid for. Some economists believe that at a level of 12 billion dollars a year they might be paid for out of an increase in the national income, especially if the interest rate can be kept as low as it is today, without adverse effect on the standard of living. Political considerations make it very unlikely that they will be paid for the wisest way. As we are committed completely to armament economics, we shall pay in a reduction of the standard of living which may be postponed but cannot be averted.

We shall pay for armament economics in the diversion or outright waste of materials useful for human comfort.

We shall probably pay in largely retrogressive taxation, including sales taxes which always fall most heavily on low income groups. This will be the case even if much more drastic legislation should be enacted to recover war or armament profits than now exists.

We shall pay for continuing armament economics, even if we escape war, by excessive inflation, one long economic jag with a hideous hangover. Experience abroad shows that we can get substantial inflation even before the army of the unemployed has been absorbed in work.

We shall pay for armament economics all too probably by war toward which the momentum of that economy tends, for armament economics is like bicycle-riding for a beginner: to stay on one must keep going. To keep going indefinitely means war.

President Roosevelt clearly stated this truth in his famous Buenos Aires speech early in 1937:

"We know, too, that vast armaments are rising on every side and that the work of creating them employs men and women by the millions. It is natural, however, to conclude that such employment is false employment, that it builds no permanent structure, and creates no consumers' goods for lasting prosperity. We know that nations guilty of these follies inevitably face the day either when their weapons of destruction must be used against their neighbors, or when an unsound economy like a house of cards will fall apart."

The most probable expectation is that a combination of all these methods of paying for long continued armament economics will lead to a chaotic crisis to which an extreme form of totalitarianism will be the answer.

In our so-called liberal magazines, the brilliant English economist, John Maynard Keynes, and those who in varying degree are his disciples, boldly or timorously, as the case may be, try to refute this melancholy conclusion. In general they argue that our unused resources of men and machines are now so large, and our possibilities for production so tremendous, that we can have both cannon and butter on a vast scale *; that armament economics may help to strike from us the shackles of a traditional finance capitalism and discover to us our power. Possibly to a limited extent this may be true, if we can assume a degree of intelligence not much in evidence. There is some encouragement in the report of the Federal Reserve Board which asks Congress to remove the President's powers of inflation, to control the evils in our present gold-purchase law, and to bring about an ultimate "balancing of the budget when full utilization of the nation's economic capacity approaches." That would mean an end of government financing by loans if and when experts might agree that the Board's conditions had been met.†

*Calvin B. Hoover in the *New York Times* of February 16, 1941, agrees that Germany under Hitler not only abolished unemployment but raised the standard of living of the masses prior to the war. But (a) this was in comparison with the low levels of 1932, and (b) it was accomplished by overall planning which America has not embraced.

† Since these paragraphs were written, I have seen Congressman Jerry Voorhis' bills for outright government ownership of the Federal Reserve Banks, and "the financing of national defense without incurring public debt" through a "debt-free credit issuance" for defense purposes to be retired out of tax levies. I favor the first bill and am inclined to favor the second. It would mean very heavy taxation and a great broadening of the income tax base.

But the Board's recommendations have not been adopted. In *Common Sense* (February 1941) Dr. Mordecai Ezekiel, able economist of the Agricultural Department, fears that they may put too much of a brake on our economic expansion. He paints a rosy and unconvincing picture of high living standards and enormous armaments without inflation. His hopes have little economic, and less political, foundation.

I think it logically possible even at this late date to shift from planning only for defense into overall planning for abundance. I think it more possible by a vast exercise of constructive imagination at the end of this war crisis to turn the facilities for armament production in orderly fashion to peacetime production. But I do not think that what is logically possible is at all probable—although I shall work for it. The war and armament mentality are against it. Armament economics wins the day because it is a type of expansion understood by private capitalists, and one from which historically they have gained much and from which they still hope to gain. They want to make the government assume the risks while they get the profits. They will not succeed this time as well as before, but they have far more hope of success along conventional lines in preserving their profits than they have from overall democratic socialization, which would emphasize abundance, and provide out of abundance for defense but not foreign wars.

It is certain that armament economics will hasten the coming of collectivism, but the motives to which it appeals and the circumstances under which it operates, heavily weight the scales in favor of communism or fascism rather than democracy.

This is particularly true because, even if we escape belligerent participation in the present war, conscript armies all dressed up, backed by enormous industries, will seek some place to go. Or rather the generals and the armament magnates, whether private employers or bureaucrats, will seek that place. In a country situated as the United States is situated, conscription and armament economics of themselves are standing invitations to imperial adventure, which we will undertake in this hemisphere in the name of its protection, and perhaps also in the rest of the world as junior partner, but now or later as rival or successor, to the British Empire.

That is, we shall probably go imperialist if we are not too exhausted by war. And the accompaniment of foreign imperialism in the next generation will not be the growth of domestic liberalism which characterized the British Empire in the nineteenth century. That was possible only under the peculiar conditions that then existed. Our imperialism to be halfway successful, practically and psychologically, will require fascist organization of the nation at home. The cost of imperial expansion will be heavy, and the reward comparatively slight. The whole nation must be regimented to the task as was not necessary in England in the days of good Queen Victoria, or in America when our ancestors easily wrested this continent from the Indians.

This drift to imperialism and fascism was emphasized and accentuated by the President's Lend-Lease Bill and the arguments of its supporters. There was no fascist intention, I think, in the bill, but as I have pointed out in Chapter IV, it did turn over the awful power of war or peace to one man. That is dictatorship and that it should be called democracy by so many argues a weak resistance to non-democratic methods if the dictator or the end he seeks is approved.

To sum up this analysis of our social trends: America drifts to fascism even if we should escape belligerent participation in war. But it is a drift against which we may successfully contend. With all its faults our democratic tradition is strong; our republic has a stability unmatched in Europe. We have neither the inferiority complex of defeat nor the natural poverty which goaded Germany along the road to Nazi dictatorship. If we keep out of war we have an excellent fighting chance for making our democracy win.

That chance is neither as surely blessed by British victory nor damned by British defeat as some of us are saying. German victory will make the world a worse and more dangerous place. But it will not give Hitler omnipotence to conquer us. If we hate Nazism as much as we say we do, we shall hardly voluntarily imitate it because of its temporary triumph abroad. Our fascism is more likely to be domestic in roots and quality. (Economically, as I hope this book will help to make clear, we cannot escape a high degree of collectivism whoever wins the war, but with our resources, especially if we maintain the friendship of this hemisphere, we can shape and control our own democratic collectivism beyond Hitler's power to make us take his brand.)

It is true that a sweeping Hitler victory will immensely complicate the struggle against armament economics. We shall probably feel that we must confront him with an armed state. That will not be equally true if Britain should be victorious, or even if Britain should gain a peace which would leave her a mighty and vigorous nation. Perhaps whoever wins, world reaction to war and world economic crisis may help give us a breathing space from war and lighten the armament burden. Even so, that burden will not be dropped—not even if miraculously there should be another British victory like that in the First World War. By that time too many American generals, admirals, munition makers and imperialists— yes, and workers—will have or think they have a stake in maintaining conscription and armament economics. It will be easy to find an enemy to fear. Stalin or his successor will be around. Even Britain may provoke our armed rivalry as after the First World War. The most bitter attack ever made upon me in public discussion came in the 'twenties from a retired rear-admiral who was sure that we had condemned ourselves to defeat not by Germany or Russia or Japan but by England when we accepted the Washington naval treaties. American imperialism, let me reiterate the fact, will not be ended by British victory.*

* In the short space of time that this manuscript was at the printers my fears of American imperialism were not only confirmed but strengthened by speeches by Paul McNutt, Henry Luce's widely publicized screed in favor of an Anglo-American empire with us as *senior* partner,

But I take great heart for the hard fight against our own fascism if we can keep out of war. If we get in, no matter with what idealistic hopes, I think the defeat of our democracy is all but sealed. Given our fascist tendencies and our lack of clarity in understanding democracy, total war fought thousands of miles from home will require totalitarianism; propaganda, censorship and conscription raised to the nth degree. The President can put the country into war; there will be acceptance of the war and outwardly, at first, but little protest. But it will be unpopular not only with the millions who think it unnecessary but with other millions who had thought we could win by sending supplies but not our sons to distant battlefields. The cost will be prodigious. A bitter people, still fighting, will seek scapegoats in truly fascist style. Smoldering race hatreds will be fanned to flames. Remember that the Ku Klux Klan of the 'twenties was born of the First World War.

I say this not from wishful thinking—with all my heart I could wish it untrue—but because I know America, and I know that what *is* cannot be altered merely by desire in the laboratory of war any more than in the chemical laboratory. Nor will democracy—which had a

and Dorothy Thompson's lyric endorsement of Mr. Luce's vision of an "American Century" rebaptized as "American Destiny." The kind of war made probable by the pursuit of this dream is more likely to lead to "Stalin's century" or a "century of exhaustion." If by a miracle we should win the power Mr. Luce covets, we should have to maintain it by a military establishment, and probably by wars great and small, at a ruinous cost. A national income that might be used to raise the standard of living would be absorbed in large part by this imperialist gamble under the direction of a fascist state.

narrow escape in the last war and the years that followed
—be so easily restored after this. Peace will come in the
end to a country which will have suffered things of
which it never dreamed in the First World War. In a
country burdened with crushing debt and caught in the
crisis of change to peacetime economy, a very strong
hand will seem the only alternative to chaos.

Such a nation as ours in such a struggle will not have
found the wisdom to give to the world that which we
ourselves will have lost. Even if the miracle of complete
victory should come to our armies, the America which
will have drunk deep of war's madness will write a worse
and stupider peace, for a greater area of the world, than
was written at Versailles.

"Charles E. Hughes was moved to question openly
'whether constitutional government as heretofore maintained in this republic could survive another great war
even victoriously waged.'" So wrote Charles A. Beard
in the September 1940 issue of *Coronet*.

Grant that these probabilities are less than certainties,
they are the stuff with which statesmen and enlight-
ened citizens must deal. No one should dare to gamble
the lives of 131 million Americans and the fate of our
democracy on the desperately slim chance of an easy
war followed by a victory for an America which will
come through with democracy unimpaired. It is an
ominous thing for that democracy that, if the Gallup
poll is right, support for possible war—as was support
for conscription—is greatest in precisely that South in
which, for historic and economic reasons, poverty is

greatest, race feeling strongest, and democracy weakest.

He who loves his country and democracy will not give up all hope even in the midst of war. But because he loves his country and democracy he will, so long as there is time, cry out that war will not banish fascism from the earth, but bring it to this last fair land where an orderly development of democracy might have blessed not only our own people, but eventually all the peoples of the earth. For what we cannot do for mankind by the violence of total war, we may yet do by example.

What we can do to achieve total democracy at home still remains for fuller study. For me that study has required as a preface specific reexamination of many of the ideas, theories, and social forces which in the years that are gone have sought my allegiance. Reappraisals must precede plan.

CHAPTER VI ☆ REAPPRAISALS

TO SOCIALISTS of the great tradition, memory adds its weight of bitterness to the tragedy of these years. Before the First World War each new day brought tidings from afar of the spread of their gospel of hope to the workers of the world. Even to the victims of despotisms not yet conquered came the assurance that their sufferings had meaning, not alone to themselves, not alone to their nation, but to that great brotherhood of the lowly of every land whose destiny was the glorious conquest of war, poverty, and every form of exploitation.

The First World War was a shock to the socialist, an interlude in his hope. But by no means its death. Jaurès was assassinated, and with him died the dream of international action by the workers to prevent that war. Yet the majority of socialists who in Germany as well as in England and France supported their respective governments, honestly sought a negotiated peace and honestly believed that they might make that war the last. The minority socialists, no small company, opposed the war and socialist participation in it, and were buoyed up along their hard road by the conviction that war itself would open the minds of the masses to socialist truth and breed the revolution which would end it.

Then came, marvel of marvels, socialist revolution in the land of the Tsars, and after a time the establishment of a social democratic government where once the Kaiser ruled. The new world drew near.

Not even the Socialist-Communist feud and the adversities of the 'twenties seemed to loyal socialists to do more than postpone the day of victory. As the 'thirties wore on, socialism's defensive position was painfully evident. And 1940 saw the Second International dissolved and democratic socialism all but destroyed on the European continent. Its morale had been broken months or years before the end. The Third International has degraded socialism to Stalinism, and, crowning indignity to Socialists, our arch enemy, Hitler, has appropriated the socialist name and coupled it in the minds of millions with the cruelties of his tribal nationalism. The American Socialist Movement, never among the strongest, has been sensitive to these fluctuations in socialist fortunes abroad, as well as to adverse conditions at home. Yet in the bitterness of our disappointment we have no time for tears; we cannot afford the luxury of despair. There is life to be lived for ourselves and our children; there are mistakes to be redeemed. If the years have taunted us with the dreams we lost, those same years have inexorably brought doom to the old order as the natural consequence of the internal contradictions and the failures which our socialist analysis had revealed. The will to live demands that we act; and constructive action must begin by adding to our analysis of the failure of capitalist-nationalism an equally fearless search for the reasons why democratic socialism has not been recognized as its heir and successor.

In this search it helps me, and therefore I dare to hope my readers, to set down my present appraisals of some of the ideas and concepts which have played so large a part in socialist—and more than socialist—thought and action.

He who desires a better social order and would help to bring that about must have some notion of the forces which move men and shape social change. Karl Marx did not entirely invent, but he clarified and emphasized the notion of *economic determinism* as a theory of history. His friend and collaborator Friedrich Engels thus summarized the theory in a famous passage:

"Marx discovered the simple fact (hitherto hidden beneath ideological overgrowths) that human beings must have food, drink, clothing and shelter first of all, before they can interest themselves in politics, science, art, religion and the like. This implies that the production of the immediately requisite material means of subsistence, and therewith the existing phase of development of a nation or an epoch, constitute the foundation upon which the state institutions, the legal outlooks, the artistic and even the religious ideas are built up. It implies that the latter must be explained out of the former, whereas the former have usually been explained as issuing from the latter."

Here is no crass and vulgar assertion that "every man has his price" and is motivated solely by considerations of economic self-interest. Neither does the theory deny the immense power of political and cultural ideas once they are established. Marx and Engels made it abundantly plain that they recognized the effect upon human institutions of what modern sociologists emphasize as the "time lag."

This Marxist theory of history has been exceedingly fruitful. But, as Max Eastman has pointed out, it has suffered in the hands of Marxists, including Marx himself, because they treated productive forces as a sufficient *explanation* of history, instead of as a primary factor *conditioning* all others. "That is to say, that no historic phenomenon can arise and endure which *runs counter* to the prevailing mode of production. This does not mean, however, that everything which arises and endures is *explained* by the prevailing mode of production." * One serious consequence of this confusion of *effective cause* with *indispensable condition* has been the Marxist tendency to ignore human psychology.

More inclusive than this theory of history and often identified with it, was Marx's larger concept of *dialectical materialism*. This, as all students with even a superficial acquaintance with Marxism are aware, is an "inverted Hegelianism." The German philosopher Hegel had taught that the whole cosmos was idea, but idea which in itself went through a continuous process of change or dialectic unfolding. All things, most clearly of all human history, are but the manifestation of the idea, let us call it the mind of God, which by logical necessity moves toward nobler truth and more perfect unity through a process of affirmation (thesis), self-contradiction (antithesis) and new formulation (synthesis).

* Max Eastman: *Marxism: Is it a Science?*, p. 25, 26ff—to which at this point I am indebted. The quotation from Engels is from his speech at the grave of Marx.

Marx, who began as a disciple of Hegel, reacted vehemently against the dominance of the idea but substituted for it a notion equally philosophic, or "religious" rather than scientific; namely, that reality consists in the evolution of material things. There is on my shelves a book by Bukharin and other Russians who, with vast learning and complete unsuccess, attempt to make their dialectical materialism an adequate metaphysical framework for all the sciences. Marx, I think, would have approved. He would have scoffed at the divinity and perhaps the remoteness of "the far off divine event" to which Tennyson saw the whole creation moving. He would have mocked the easy road to it which social evolutionists of the optimistic years foresaw, but he was equally sure of the certainty of his goal. Loyalty to this creed of the master has made lesser Marxists barren and bitter theologians who worship at the shrine of a dialectic which is helpful only when it is treated as one method useful in the search for truth. We need a better, not a worse, science of human history and conduct than Marx gave us. But that science cannot omit, as did Marx's—and even more conspicuously Lenin's—frank recognition of and appeal to human values.

The *class conflict* concept which has played so great a rôle in Marxist socialism fits beautifully into Marx's theory of history and his dialectical materialism. Nevertheless, it has independent support on the basis of observed phenomena, past and present. It scarcely needs argument that human society is characterized by many class or group conflicts and that historic changes have arisen from those conflicts. I should go farther and agree, now as always, that despite a confusion of groups and a blurring of lines of division by contradictory loyalties, *the* class conflict is derived from the economic situation, and that in our time it is based on the difference in interest between those who own productive property and think of themselves primarily as owners, and those who have only their labor to sell. It by no means follows that instinctive realization of that fact infallibly unites each side to the conflict in unity against the other, or that out of conflicts which take roughly a class pattern wisdom is born to build a classless world. Every day's news illustrates both the existence of class conflict and its lack of simplicity or clear direction. Hitler, the bitter enemy of Marxism, now talks of "the world of labor" against "the world of gold." Messrs. Willkie and Roosevelt, both of whom deplore and reject the class-conflict theory, would have a hard time explaining the nature of their own support in the recent campaign except with the aid of an instinctive class feeling, largely independent of pure or applied reason. And Stalin would have an even harder time proving that in the U.S.S.R. class conflict had operated under the guidance of the Bolshevik élite to produce a genuinely classless society.

As a practical matter here in America, I think everything is to be gained by emphasizing the rôle of the workers, and the rights of the workers in the fullest sense of the term "worker." I think nothing is to be gained and something lost by making faith in the class struggle the cardinal principle of socialist thought and action. And that, briefly, for the following reasons:

Here in America we are dealing with a public which, including wage workers as well as working farmers, technicians, engineers and professional men, thinks of itself to an amazing degree as "middle class"—as is revealed in, for instance, the *Fortune* Survey of February 1940. The beginning of its effective education for a co-operative commonwealth is not an insistence on the primacy of a class conflict along lines which it by no means consciously accepts. If, as in much popular Marxism, the working class is interpreted narrowly as wage workers to whom everybody else is set in opposition, the cause is lost before the battle is fairly joined. Or if it should be ultimately won, it would be at a cost society cannot afford to pay. In the name of class conflict Russian communism wiped out not only its capitalists, but its engineers, managers and technicians. Painfully it had to replace them, and in the process it has acquired a new class of bureaucrats and managers no more sympathetic to the workers than the old. For this result millions of plain people have starved.

That brilliant writer, Harold Laski, who has never reconciled, as I think he might, his original political pluralism with his later zeal for Marx, in his *Parliamentary Government* presents a completely unresolved contradiction between nostaglic affection for familiar British institutions, including the Crown, and the conviction that they simply can't work, once the masses are awake to the grim realities of class conflict. He overlooks the one fact that possibly in Britain, even without the incalculable effects of the present war, might have permitted a solution of this conflict. It is a fact even more apparent in our America. I refer to the technological progress which makes it possible with intelligence and good will to produce so much that almost immediately all but a relatively very small number of the rich would be better off in terms of security and actual satisfaction of wants than they are amid today's uncertainties and conflicts. This will by no means be true if the establishment of the new order requires bitter violence.

Clearly, then, to get what we want with a minimum of destruction both of order and liberty requires emphasis on what ought to unite us, or what we can do together, in the society we might win, not on the divisions which breed hate. To recognize the existence of the class conflict is helpful especially if it stimulates us to remove its causes. But to believe that the stimulation of instinctive class hate, alongside of, or instead of, national and racial hate, will save mankind is madness. There is, alas, all too much reason for believing in the power of hate in the record of what both Lenin and Hitler have done by their varying appeals to it. But if we must use it, can we not employ it against forces and institutions rather than men; against the "soullessness"—to use a good old-fashioned term—of those fictional "persons," great corporations, rather than against "international Jewish bankers" or even wicked capitalists; against war rather than the soldiers who fight it? And always with the determination that we destroy only to make way for some institution which can better serve a fellow-ship of free men. Today the number of us who would be better off in body, mind and spirit by a different or-dering of our society is so overwhelming that with intel-ligent cooperation we could make the opposition of a tiny, selfish and stupid minority inconsequential!

What I have been saying bears upon the whole no-tion of *revolution*. If that is to be understood in the popular sense of civil war, it is an enormous evil, most of all in these days when war can be so destructive. Of all wars, civil wars are the worst in the suffering they entail and the harm they do to normal human relations. A man's foes become those of his own household. "Fifth columns" at home are more ubiquitous and terrible than foreign foes.

As a matter of fact, it is romantic nonsense today to dream of successful *violent* revolution of the masses against a government which still holds the loyalty of the soldiers who operate not ordinary guns, but bombers and tanks and artillery. If these favor the revolutionists, their cause is won. Both Mussolini and Hitler probably set the pattern for successful revolution even of a violent sort. Their violence fell short of armed insurrection; they used existing state machinery. There is still, I think, some validity in the socialist hope of turning inter-national war into revolution, but the success of that sort of revolution will depend upon its usefulness in stopping war at home and abroad. The revolutionary effort cannot even be made in a military sense except with a very unpopular war like the First World War in Russia, or, as one begins to hope, in the Second World War in Mussolini's Italy.

But there is another and truer sense in which the concept of revolution is valuable. Perhaps some genius will invent a name for it free from the overtones of war and terrorism, but the reality behind the word as I mean it is indispensable. If we are to be saved there is need of sharp and conscious change in our social purpose and direction, and that is revolution. Society is never truly static. The tempo of change in a machine age is very rapid. An evolutionary approach to that change can do something. But there is no painless process of creation. We may find ourselves in a collectivist society almost unawares. But not in a society which can be called a fellowship of free men. Any *program* of social action must be more or less gradual, however revolutionary its goal. The more violent it is in our modern close-knit society the slower will be the process of construction. But a creative program requires a creative purpose, and that, in turn, in a world caught in slavery to outworn loyalties, requires an act of conversion the political equivalent of which is revolution. It cannot come without struggle, without pain of thinking and labor of action. But the less violent the struggle, the more revolutionary may be its quality.

This discussion of familiar concepts has, perhaps, suggested to the reader my attitude toward *the historical rôle of the workers*, but the matter requires further discussion. I am still of the opinion, which I have repeated times without number, that it is the exploited who must be the principal authors of their own emancipation if it is to be secure. The very conditions of their work give the employees of mines and factories training and opportunity for mass action. More than that, the future success of the good society requires emphasis on the dignity of labor. Able-bodied adults must live by honorable work of hand and brain for which our economic system will no longer deny them opportunity. Only so can the great adventure of human life and progress succeed. It is the ideals of *workers*, not of *owners* upon which the moral foundations of any good society must be built.

Hence my criticism of the recent tendency to see in the middle class *as such* a great vehicle of progress. Of course we cannot neglect and flout it as socialist parties in some times and places have rather ostentatiously done —this despite the fact that the great majority of socialist leaders have sprung from the middle class. The middle class, sociologically speaking, contains today too many indispensable workers, farmers, technicians and others. But its usefulness depends upon its consciousness of honorable productive function, not upon a caste pride in social status based primarily on possession of property.

But thus to exalt workers and work is a very different thing from believing that the wage-earning proletariat is by its nature and destiny society's Messiah. The history of revolutionary change in country after country in Europe gives the lie to that hope. For good and evil it was not Russia's working masses but the Bolshevik "élite" who manipulated both peasants and wage workers to shape the pattern of life in the U.S.S.R. where, under flattery and coercion, the masses have accepted a new slavery for the old with disheartening docility. The history of the failure of the proletariat during a revolutionary situation differs in different lands, but always there has been failure. Those labor parties have fared best which, as in Britain, have attracted important middle class elements or, as in Scandinavia, have developed a working alliance with the farmers. "Workers of the world, unite" is still one of the noblest of slogans, but to be effective it cannot be based on the simple statement that those who should unite have literally "nothing to lose but your chains."

Today one merely stresses the obvious to insist that the decay of private capitalism has not reduced almost all the vital elements of the population to the economic or psychological status of propertyless proletarians. Nor can wage workers either dispense with or spontaneously supply the engineers, technicians, managers, or farmers necessary to the maintenance of machine-age society. Moreover, precisely because workers need above all things jobs for daily bread, or some grant of a modicum of bread if they are without jobs, they are essentially conservative, fearful of too great risk, willing to take even a little "bird in the hand," ready to act drastically only in crisis. And crisis in the modern world of specialization and integration cannot today be resolved in terms simply of revolt.

These facts still require that labor, organized in its own unions and consumers' cooperatives, and prepared for effective political action, play an essential rôle in building the cooperative commonwealth as the alternative to the totalitarian state. But it cannot be said that the present state of labor organization in America encourages hope in its adequacy for the crisis.

As I look back on the years nothing gives me more satisfaction than what I have been able to do to vindicate in behalf of the workers the right to organize, and to help them exercise it. There is no more essential civil liberty under democracy. And no unknown soldiers have ever served mankind better than the largely anonymous heroes of labor's struggle for its own independent organization. The extension of such organization and the spread of collective bargaining are among the major achievements of the New Deal, achievements impossible, of course, without labor's own heroic efforts. What a great labor union can mean to its own members in more than higher wages and shorter hours is to be seen in the heart-warming cultural and educational activities of the International Ladies Garment Workers Union.

Nevertheless, a clever politician could probably win great success by a campaign for government regulation of unions and the protection of workers, organized and unorganized, from labor's own bureaucracies. He could certainly win support from Negroes to end the trade-union's exclusion of them or discrimination against them which is still widespread. On the average, the rights of workers as citizens of the state, at least up to the war crisis, have been better protected in the United States than their rights as members of their own unions. The legal and extra-legal powers of trade-union presidents and executive boards arbitrarily to discipline members they don't like is excessive. Inner democracy is as badly protected in Sidney Hillman's supposedly progressive Amalgamated Clothing Workers of America as in some of the A.F. of L. building trades. And that is saying a great deal. Increasingly workers are resorting to the civil courts to protect their right to work at their own trades, a right denied to them as the result of union "discipline," sometimes utterly without trial, sometimes with farcical trial. (It must be remembered that the more closed shop agreements there are, the more serious a punishment is expulsion from the union.) The extreme form of despotism in unions is found where racketeers are in control.

Racketeering, which is rampant in certain unions, especially in certain great cities, is beginning to attract public attention, thanks to Westbrook Pegler and others. This disease, which takes toll to the tune of millions of dollars annually, originated with business and the pursuit of profit, not with labor. But the American tendency to violence in group disputes gave the merchants of violence a rare opportunity to "muscle in" on the labor field where racketeers function: (1) to exploit both employers and workers; (2) very often to keep in power over the union officials who belong to the gang or will pay tribute to it; and (3) to hold consumers in line while employers and labor bosses jointly rob them. The ominous feature of the situation is not so much that racketeers have often forced their way into the labor union field—that is a reflection of certain phases of American life—but that there is so little disposition and power among the workers to clean their own house.

Rank and file workers do not like racketeers, but if the racketeers in charge of their unions, or employed by their bureaucrats, render or seem to render service by "protecting them" or winning them better wages under semi-monopolistic conditions, they prefer not to take the risks—often very real—of fighting their gun-toting exploiters. A local labor leader of vision and ideals in one of the building trades was telling me bitterly of the failure of a fight against racketeering which he had led. He particularly bemoaned the ease with which men who began as radicals and reformers fell in with racketeering. He commented even more bitterly on the control over building which the highly autocratic officials of the small but essential operating engineers' union had acquired by practices which made them, as he said, racketeers and parasites. He saw no reform in sight save perhaps by government prosecution, to him a dangerous weapon. Finally, he said that despite the official A.F. of L. resolution against peacetime conscription the majority of the members in his big local welcomed it as making work for them, particularly by getting the young fellows out of the way.

His pessimism was expressed after the A.F. of L. had passed a pious and toothless resolution condemning racketeering. For bringing up the subject at all, President David Dubinsky of the I.L.G.W.U. had been physically attacked by one Joseph Fay, an important figure in New Jersey A.F. of L. circles. During my fight against Mayor Frank Hague of Jersey City when that boss's machine instigated a riot at my meeting in Military Park in Newark, it was Mr. Fay, according to the press, who persuaded the A.F. of L. Trades and Labor Assembly of Essex County to reject a resolution condemning the riot in favor of one praising the police who had handled it so badly that they were later condemned by an official investigation of the Police Department. Throughout the struggle for free speech in Jersey, partly because the C.I.O. led it, partly because of the tie-up between Hague and the labor bosses, the A.F. of L. unions of the district, with a few important exceptions, actually supported Hague's position. When I called evidences of this to the attention of President William Green of the A.F. of L., who in principle always approves of civil liberty, he almost frantically repudiated accurate knowledge of the situation, responsibility for its evils, or power to deal with it. This is his characteristic attitude on racketeering, lack of democracy, discrimination against Negroes and other abuses when called to his attention. It is his weakness as much as his personal respectability which makes him so satisfactory a president for the tough-minded oligarchs who control the Executive Council of the great A.F. of L. on terms about as unidealistic as any capitalist venture.

The C.I.O. at its inception had more vision, genuine desire to organize the unorganized, and a more realistic conception of the necessity for industrial rather than craft organization in the mass-production industries. As the years passed, it suffered from the faults of the man

116

whose strength was originally one of its great assets. John L. Lewis for personal reasons, many labor men believe, lost a chance for highly desirable labor unity when it was possible on reasonable terms. He became too much subject to Communist influence—perhaps without realizing it. Still later his judgment was marred by his extraordinary jealousy of President Roosevelt. There is no other satisfactory explanation of his support of Mr. Willkie against the will of the overwhelming majority of his own organization.

His renunciation of the presidency of the C.I.O. still leaves him a power in it for he is still head of the United Mine Workers. So, too, are his allies, the Communists and near-Communists, a power in the organization. They have shown themselves often more devoted as organizers than the old line A.F. of L. men, but on occasion as unscrupulous in political method as the worst of them. What makes the Communist influence serious is not that communism is "radical"; it is that Communist action in unions is absolutely controlled from without, in the last analysis, by none other than Stalin, with primary reference not to the needs of organized labor in America, or to a fraternal and democratic internationalism, but to Stalin's red imperialism. That is true in every civic organization in which Communists act. And they are past masters in the tricks by which organized minorities can control majorities. Philip Murray, the able new president of the C.I.O. has a man-size job on his hands.

One of the failures of the American labor movement is in leadership. It has developed able and honest business executives and efficient and devoted organizers, but few men who can sweep it along in social action with vision and power. There is probably no leader as popular or as trusted even in his own union as are at least three outstanding political figures: President Roosevelt, Senator Wagner of New York, and Senator La Follette of Wisconsin. At least, the labor leader couldn't get so many of his workers' votes for public office. The comparison is not quite fair because the executive job in a union arouses irritations which the political figure can avoid, inasmuch as labor at present demands relatively little of its political friends. Nevertheless I shall not soon forget the unanimous answer I received in the Pennsylvania anthracite region to my inquiries, at the height of Mr. Lewis's labor popularity, whether his support had not meant a great deal to the President. "Hell no, John owes a lot more to Roosevelt for his support." And certainly it is true that the great increase of union membership in recent years is more largely due to the Wagner Labor Act, and a friendly administration in Washington, than to the vision and energy of the great labor organizations and their leaders. The peace between the A.F. of L. and C.I.O., which is wanted by so many of the more thoughtful workers who know how costly has been the civil war between them, is more likely to be the consequence of political pressures at a time of absorption in national defense than to come from labor statesmanship.

This may in itself not prevent peace from blessing the workers, but there are limits beyond which dependence upon government action to heal labor's disastrous divisions, prosecute racketeers, protect individual rights, and prevent race discrimination in unions will threaten their vitality as independent agencies of progress, and make it easy to reduce them to company unions in relation to the government. Certainly it is sheer romanticism to expect from the union movement *as such* any real purification and advancement of democracy within the political state unless and until it has more perfectly vindicated its own democracy. It is possible that an American dictator will not have to smash a labor union movement as did Mussolini and Hitler because he will already have harnessed it to his chariot of power.

This is one of the reasons why reluctantly I have abandoned hope for a *labor party* as an answer to our problem of political realignment. Another reason is the complete undesirability of control of a political party by labor unions as such. (According to *Fortune's* surveys, during 1940 only 11.4 per cent of the workers thought well of a labor party. But then, according to the same survey, only a quarter of the factory workers thought of themselves as belonging to the working class, and the workers were very skeptical of the management of the unions.) No labor party of any sort, indeed no progressive party, can be as strong as it ought without sympathetic support from organized labor and organized farmers. But that support, to be politically effective, must be based on recognition of the different rôles of unions and political parties. Save under exceptional conditions, the active efforts of labor unions and their chiefs must be confined to the immediate interests of the union movement, usually of a particular union in the struggle for better conditions. Political parties are or should be vehicles for wider social plans. Political action, in the narrow sense, to be effective against a strong class interest needs to be backed by organized labor with its potential economic power. But a society trying to work out its problems in a time of revolutionary change won't get far if the radical or progressive labor party is primarily the instrument of labor unions in their day-by-day struggle.

This risk, I used to argue, could be averted by the right type of labor party organization. So it could. But in the present state of American public opinion and labor organization any labor party emphasizing that name would be, or soon become, a trade-union party with limited appeal.

One factor which hinders the building of a sound labor party is the nature of Communist activity. The American Labor Party in New York State, for which I once had considerable hope, has required the continual intervention of trade-union leaders to prevent its capture by the organized Communists within it. Their success has not been complete but, such as it is, it was greatly aided by the magic of Roosevelt's name. The anti-Communists said, "Support us to support Roosevelt." Now, as the voting record shows, about 425,000 people in New York preferred to vote for Roosevelt under the A.L.P. rather than the Democratic label. All of them could have voted for Roosevelt—and Senator Mead—anyhow. The A.L.P. helped elect candidates of the old parties whom it endorsed. In New York City it elected none solely its own. It has two councilmen elected under proportional representation, one of them the well known Socialist, Harry W. Laidler. Its future for an indefinite period under non-Communist or perhaps under disguised Communist control, will be as a bargaining, balance-of-power group. It has shown little capacity to develop and promote great social ideas or a far-reaching social program; it has developed no significant leadership of its own. This is true of every attempt—and there have been many—for a labor party in America. Altogether they have been of no such influence in the realm of ideas and programs as the little Socialist Party; they have not shown such power of survival; they have not developed political leaders of anything like the stature of the older Socialists, Gene Debs, Morris Hillquit, Victor Berger, Meyer London, James Maurer, and Dan Hoan. It is significant that the La Follettes in Wisconsin have carefully avoided membership in the Progressive Farmer-Labor Federation (which itself recently dropped the Farmer-Labor part of its name) and which operates none too satisfactorily under the primary laws within the Progressive Party.

Of all the state labor parties which have been projected or tried except the A.L.P. in New York State, only the Minnesota Farmer-Labor Party is still alive and strong. It has developed as yet no leader with the strength to take the place of its colorful chief, Governor Floyd Olson, who died in office.

In brief, I see less sign of the healthy spread of the

right sort of labor party than at almost any time since the Socialist Party endorsed the idea early in the 'twenties, and indicated its desire under certain conditions to merge with it for purposes of electoral action. A nation-wide farmer-labor party of the right sort is today for me another lost hope.

There is, however, one more brief observation which is in order in any reappraisal of the concepts and forces with which we must deal. Recent years have given me no cause to modify my condemnation of *organized Communism* in America, but much to add to my concern over certain human qualities which its history reveals. It still enlists amazing devotion to the service of a complete Machiavellianism. It glorifies deceit. It is the first radical or revolutionary organization which has made it a rule and a virtue for its members (except those who have to function publicly for it) to deny their membership in a party which they serve fanatically. No agreement with them for cooperation for specific purposes—as labor men and Socialists, myself among them, have learned to our sorrow—is worth anything at any time or place where it conflicts with the party bureaucracy's judgment of its own interests. Falsehood and slander are its characteristic weapons in their factional quarrels. The human traits thus exalted would turn any economic paradise into a hell even assuming that such a paradise could be achieved.

What astonishes and disturbs me is the continuing strength of Communism. I could well understand it under its united-front program when in America the party functioned in certain aspects as an extreme left wing of the New Deal. But at the end of August 1939 it was obliged by the Hitler-Stalin Pact to change its mind over night on the vital issue of foreign policy; to bless what it had cursed, and curse what it had blessed. In the process it lost some members and perhaps a majority of its fellow travellers. It was by no means broken. It still commands undivided allegiance from its followers who will stay with it in the not impossible event that Stalin should order it again to change its line, and bless American entry into a war it now opposes, in order to defeat a Japan with whom the Russian dictator has reached no understanding.

What is equally or perhaps even more amazing and disquieting is the fact that throughout Stalin's régime, otherwise excellent people, not only communists but liberals, intellectuals, or what you will, have used standards of judgment on Russia and Russian affairs entirely different from those applied to any other part of the world. Effective social action toward a good society has been gravely hindered because trusted reporters so seriously misled radical and progressive opinion on what was happening in the U.S.S.R., and because even when at last facts about Stalin's rule, its man-made famine, its purges, its invasion of Finland had to be admitted, they were interpreted so that vice became virtue; cruelty, firmness; and black, white. In spite of crimes entirely similar to Hitler's in cruelty, and even more extensive, Stalin still appears a light and a leader to thousands of generally well meaning Americans.

At no point has the sterility or worse of a large section

of the self-styled American intelligentsia been more evident than here. Look at its record: extravagant support of Wilson's war to make the world safe for democracy; extravagant abuse of him and the other "old men of Versailles" for their failure; hesitant defense of Russian communism in the days of its hope under Lenin; wholly unwarranted enthusiasm for it under Stalin. This group of intellectuals praised democracy in the years 1914–1920; they not only criticized it but ridiculed it in the 'twenties, turning to an increasing fondness for an impossible type of dictatorship of the proletariat in the early 'thirties. Then they applauded Stalin's united front for democracy, turning against him—and then, not all of them—only after August 1939. Most of these years they have been anti-moralists and critics of religion, feeding themselves on a weird mixture of Freud and Marx, diluted to taste. Now most of them, in contemplation of Hitler, talk like rigid moralists and profess enthusiasm for a war in which other people—for few of them will be drafted—will die for Christianity. (They do not, however, throng our churches.) During most of the years between the great wars they deplored war like convinced pacifists—except possibly revolutionary wars; now they denounce the softness of youth, its "pacifist sentimentalism" or its "cynicism about ideals" and its lack of desire for participation in wholesale homicide. America is full of college professors ready to fight for ideals, variously stated, to the last drop of blood of the last undergraduate. From whatever sources we may look for the salvation of our democracy, it is not from this type of intellectuals, their conversation, their writings, or their favorite journals of opinion. (I hasten to say that I think that the *New Republic* and *Nation* are better than this composite picture of a group or tendency. But they have a great capacity for being pontifically wrong.)

Far more important than the question of what we may expect from the intellectuals is the question of what we may expect from *human nature*—which is to say, from ourselves and people like us. Certainly not perfection. The list of human faults and failings is long, dreary, and familiar reading. Man has a tragic capacity to frustrate his own noblest ambitions. But if God is disappointed in us so must be the devil. We have managed to do some remarkable things, to create beauty and achieve comradeship. Just when one is most pessimistic comes evidence to feed the light of hope even in the dark night of a world seemingly set upon destruction. Loyalty and courage are not rare virtues. We have even shown some ability to think constructively, unusual and painful as is the process.

Perhaps our most calamitous failure is our failure to know our own strength and weakness and to plan accordingly. We are so much more skilful in using materials, wood, steel, sand, stone, and using them as we ought, with recognition of their limitations, than we are in using our own passions and abilities. We know our deep-seated tendency to act as a herd, but we show little skill in those social arrangements and techniques by which we might protect ourselves from ourselves. Perhaps we might learn.

We shall not learn automatically as the result merely of an economic process. We are more than "economic men." For instance, the family which has no such function as an economic unity as in covered wagon days, shows every tendency to survive despite Reno. And we are entirely unlikely to live, most of us, in well furnished barracks or communistic colonies merely because theoretically they are more efficient. Fortunately we can produce so much that we can afford our own kitchens and homes and gardens without robbing anybody. We can get along very comfortably with a degree of cooperation far removed from the regimentation of the beehive or ant hill. In fact most of us would drive one another mad in the process of achieving or maintaining an imitation of the ant to the degree which has seemed desirable to many religious communists and other utopians.

The result of these reflections on ourselves and our organizing ideals, concepts and institutions, is that I believe that *democracy* has a chance, and not only that but a far better chance, to give us a good society than any competing ideal or system.

Yet I am profoundly distrustful of the current concept and clamorous eulogy of democracy as increasingly hypocritical and fetishistic. All our judgments of value, it seems, must be comprised under two heads: "democratic," "anti-democratic." I am inclined to think that our fascism not only will call itself anti-fascism but will claim that it is democratic. Or perhaps we shall see a dangerous revulsion against an idea so badly served in action.

Now the great virtue of democracy is not that it does not make mistakes, but that it can correct them. Its least important recommendation is that it decides issues by counting noses rather than breaking heads (although there is something to be said for the less messy process). Far more important is its insistence that government exists to serve men, not men to serve government. Thomas Mann is right that its spiritual principle is the dignity of the individual. Democracy degenerates into mobocracy, or falls prey to the dictator unless it guarantees certain rights to individuals. It cannot exist at all except as it sees to it that a minority may become a majority through persuasion.

It is entirely true that democracy as we know it, most of all in America, grew up with the system of private capitalism; its faults and hypocrisies are in large degree results of that alliance; it may die with private capitalism unless it develops creative power to deal with unemployment and unnecessary poverty. The existence of immense underprivileged groups to be bribed by bread and circuses is a standing invitation to dictatorship. Our political machines heretofore have functioned as brokers between urban masses with the vote and little else, and the classes with power and property. They have degraded but not destroyed our democracy. Today they are inadequate to the magnitude of the present problem. The enthusiasts for the California plan of "thirty dollars every Thursday" would have told us with complete subjective sincerity that they were believers in democracy. Yet the referendum which they supported would have created a state within a state, a state relatively free from our usual democratic controls, in order to pay this sum. That referendum was defeated but its direction was prophetic.

I agree entirely with those who say (and erroneously believe that they are thereby refuting socialism) that democracy depends upon the diffusion of private property. Democracy fails today because under a declining private capitalism *relatively* it gives even less of the property that means security, dignity, and some sense of power, to the masses than it seemed to be giving under an expanding capitalism before the First World War. How we can get enough wealth, how we shall divide it, what can be social, what must be individual—that will be a major inquiry in this book.

But first there is one important theoretical objection to democracy which we have already noticed in discussing class conflict but which deserves the emphasis of restatement: It is that democracy has functioned only within the framework of common ideals, beliefs and loyalties, that it depends upon almost universal acceptance of capitalism, nationalism, a republican form of government as in America, or a constitutional monarchy in England; that it cannot resolve great social and economic conflicts; for example, chattel slavery in America was settled by war. Bitter conflict in interests cannot be confined within the rules and appeased by the compromises upon which democracy depends.

In this contention there is so much truth that no one can positively predict the endurance of American democracy through our critical transition period. Certainly it will die in any great war in Europe or Asia—or in violent revolution at home. Its hope lies in two facts: (1) The transition period, properly managed, under our immense powers of production need result in extremely little economic suffering even among the classes which now think of themselves as privileged. We cannot too often insist that a successful democracy must exalt the unifying ideals of plenty, peace and freedom for all and develop plans for achieving them rapidly. (2) Democracy, even in an imperfect form, so long as it exalts tolerance and preserves civil liberty, has immediate values worth preserving during a blundering period of economic readjustment.

This is the more evident from an examination of the alternatives. Our democracy, no more than the French, can be saved in a static form by a mere sense of moral superiority. But an examination of rival new schemes is helpful.

Only two have appeared and been tried since the First World War, "the dictatorship of the proletariat" and "the government of the élite." The former was emphasized in the U.S.S.R.; the latter in Italy and more especially in Germany.

In practice the dictatorship of the proletariat is a dictatorship *over* the proletariat—and everybody else—by a Bolshevik élite who today have been reduced by violence to Stalin's yes-men. Perhaps the "backwardness" and "Asiatic" quality of the U.S.S.R. contributed to the cruelty of the process in that great land. But something of the sort is everyhere to be expected under the theory. Dictatorship requires dictators. No metaphysical quality makes "the working class" a unity for dictation. A democracy of workers is not a dictatorship in any common-sense use of words. There might be a logical case in crisis for excluding "bitter class enemies" from the right to vote—which is all that some radicals thought they meant by dictatorship of the proletariat. But that can hardly be done without violent revolution; to announce the intention of it in advance is to invite repression to prevent it. Moreover the power to exclude these enemies requires someone to judge who they are, and class enemies and personal enemies and rivals are easily lumped together. To emphasize the moral and social values of a *democracy of workers* with hand and brain, it is no help to talk about dictatorship, especially after the Russian experience. The right of every government to deal firmly with overt acts is better protection against "class enemies" than wholesale denial of citizenship based on dubious definitions of who are the enemies.

As for government by the élite, communist or fascist, who deny the people the right to rule, but who rule in the name of the working class or the nation, and, they say, for its sole benefit, one could make a strong theoretical argument save for two immense difficulties: (1) No one has found a way to pick a true élite except in terms of force, a glorification of the process by which Al Capone's gang was certainly to be numbered among the élite of Chicago. It met, for a considerable time, the test of efficient use of power. (2) No one can guarantee that the élite in power (even if these are several grades above Capone's gang) will resist the enormous corruption of power, especially when the idea of power is not subordinated to the democratic concept and controlled by some effective popular check.

What has been partially true, and can be made truer, is this: democracy better than dictatorship can provide the atmosphere and the processes for the emergence of the competent to leadership, not dictatorship. It will not be easy. The masses can be fooled; they help to fool themselves. We men often exalt mediocrity to office because we thus honor our own average abilities; we hate to think; and only rarely do we prefer death to loss of liberty. And yet man has come a long way. His journey is not ended. And democracy, at its best, is his noblest dream. It deserves to be the total and not the partial principle of his social organization.

CHAPTER VII ☆ A PLAN IN OUTLINE

IN PLANNING for our future we Americans have advantages we are inclined to forget. We know what we want; we know that we have the material resources, the mechanical power, and the skill to produce it.

No technical plan is as important as the conviction which must inspire and sustain us in working it out. That conviction is very simple: It is that we can use, for life and abundance for all, the resources and machinery which we now use for death and destruction. The basis of this conviction is in the highest degree scientific; so must be its interpretation and application. But the experimental approach which is necessary can be sustained only by a conviction religious in its quality and intensity. Men must believe in this war for total democracy against poverty and exploitation, and expect its success despite backsets and errors, with something of that quality of steadfast devotion which the inhabitants of London's East Side slums have shown in the defense of a country where their stake has been so little. I cannot too earnestly insist: It is our old loyalties and the institutions based upon them which have failed; the beginning of our hope lies in our ability to formulate adequate loyalties and scientifically to work out the institutions appropriate to them.

We must produce more, share it more equitably, and in the process add to, not subtract from, the dignity of the individual. The problem in its essence is as simple as that. We are interested primarily in abundance for all, neither in economic individualism nor collectivism save as they minister to our end. To fight about the tools wherewith we pioneers of the future may build tomorrow's world is logically as silly as would have been a war of our ancestors concerning the best plow wherewith to break the prairie.

In shaping our progress, we have the advantage of considerable knowledge of what won't work or what hasn't worked. It is a knowledge too often neglected by enthusiasts. The failure of private capitalism is painfully obvious. A natural reaction to it has been a revival of interest in utopias, old and new. For years I counted the day lost whose mail brought me no new plan to save the world, most of them fantastic.

Short of complete utopias, the faith of men is most often vested in some new form of government, usually the rule of an élite, or in some single change like monetary reform, or a lavish pension for elder citizens. We shall be saved by no élite; neither shall we be saved by any simple formula. It is not only the "automatic equilibrium" of laissez-faire theorists which has failed, but also some celebrated formulas of social reform which have been proved inadequate. Yet they are suggestive and I acknowledge my indebtedness to, as well as disagreement with, Henry George, Silvio Gessell, Major Douglas, and the Technocrats.

Our stock-taking must include reference to devices already worked out which we can use more extensively. One of the most valuable is consumers' cooperation which at last makes noteworthy headway in the United States as it has done for several generations in Europe. Consumers' cooperatives have a great rôle, not only in educating us for a new society and in helping us to achieve it, but within the new society itself as an alternative to state corporations, or as supplementary to them —as, for example, today in the field of rural electrification. The sentimental cooperators who so often ask me at forums whether consumers' cooperatives will not solve all our problems would destroy the peculiar virtue of their own organizations; namely, their voluntary nature. A municipal commission or corporation is certainly better adapted to the management of New York subways than a compulsory, or virtually compulsory, cooperative of subway riders.

Nowadays there is no escaping from the fact that control over the state apparatus has to be won and used intelligently in solving our economic and political problems. Certainly the great strength of consumers' cooperatives in Europe has not of itself solved the problem of poverty; far less the problem of war. Nevertheless consumers' cooperatives are among our definite assets in planning for social control which will not lead to the despotism of the totalitarian state.

We have other techniques of importance in building the structure of the new society. The first of these is the device of the state corporation, already in successful use in a great number of fields. I mean, of course, a corporation, ownership of which is vested in the state, but which functions as a corporation for specific purposes, using the techniques to which we have become accustomed, but not amassing profits for absentee owners. Such corporations permit a wide divorce between social ownership and general social direction on the one hand, and bureaucratic or narrowly partisan political control by the state on the other. They also permit very interesting developments in functional self-government—or self-administration.

The governing committees or boards of directors should be chosen to represent not absentee owners, but consumers on the one hand, and the workers, including the technicians in the industry, on the other.* Theirs are the continuing interests which will endure while society lasts. And they will never be made completely identical by any formula of ownership. The more general interest is the consuming interest. We work to live, not live to work. Therefore, the consumers' interest should hold the majority of votes, but the interest of those who invest their lives, their muscle and brain in the enterprise should also have direct representation. Decisions made after discussion would by no means always follow a line of division between the groups represented.

There is a lot to be said in favor of the Post Office as a public enterprise. No one in his senses would turn its functions over to the Railway Express Agency, or any private corporation. But the Post Office is not a model on which a society which would escape the dangers of

* Some advocates of public corporations would have the political state as such represented as a third interest on the boards of directors. In most cases I should oppose this plan. The state has enough power of general control without direct representatives on the directorates.

bureaucracy and totalitarianism will pattern its social control. Public corporations, patterned to fit the needs of each publicly owned enterprise, offer us far more hope. Not only can we keep the corporate form of organization and give it a soul; we can also keep familiar methods of statistical forecasting of wants and needs, the price system, and cost-accounting, and make them minister to our convenience rather than to the dominion of private profit over us.

Economists like Oskar Lange, Eduard Heinmann, H. D. Dickinson, and others have pretty well disposed of arguments to the contrary. To achieve an economy of abundance and abolish the scarcity inherent in the dominion of private ownership and operation of economic system for private profit, it is no more necessary or desirable to smash certain economic mechanisms well established in practice than it is to smash mills and factories. Both have been used to exploit men; both can be used in a free society under democratic control. And so to our plan.

LAND, including the minerals in it, and the forests on it, is still the basis for the supply of all our needs. On it and by it man must live. The defense of its private ownership by individuals and corporations is (1) that men deeply crave land they can call their own; and (2) that collective ownership and use of land on any large scale in modern times has been maintained only by continuing force, as in Russia at a cost society cannot and should not afford.

But if our present system is supposed to promote the

state of Biblical bliss achieved when every man lives under "his own vine and fig tree" it is a sorry failure. In the last state to be opened to homesteaders, Oklahoma, more than 50 per cent of the farms are run by tenants who make little either for themselves or for the absentee landlords. California is known for its "factories in the fields," the plantation system for the cultivation of cotton is responsible for the lowest level of cultural and economic well-being in America, and one of the lowest in the world. True enough, agricultural poverty in America has other roots than private landlordism. So, too, has the poverty of city slums. But that fact does not invalidate Henry George's classic criticism of allowing individual landlords to take to themselves values in the form of rent which are a social creation. And his remedy of expropriating by a tax the economic rental value of land in behalf of the society which has created it is both just and useful. It is not, however, an adequate panacea. To apply it to mineral lands might encourage an exploitation of them which would be socially detrimental. Now that the decline both in the rate of increase of population and of the foreign market for our agricultural products has ended, or greatly checked America's long real estate boom, many cities face the problem of readjusting land values and, in large areas, abolishing overassessment. Mortgage companies and the city government have had a common interest in maintaining, in false hope, land assessments originally based on the capitalization of congestion which their spokesmen publicly deplore.

The abolition of our slums cannot be achieved simply by the single tax on land. It requires large-scale planning and, until the wage structure is radically revised upward, actual subsidy of housing for low-income groups. That necessitates positive government action. So does zoning in cities and suburban areas, and the struggle against soil erosion on the farm lands. But all these difficult jobs will be more easily accomplished if there is no longer a numerous and very vocal class of landlords, most of them absentee owners who hope to gain by appropriating the rental value of the land they "own" or by acquiring the "unearned increment" of its sale under speculative conditions. Yet the principle of the tax on the rental value of land actually encourages the home owner and the farmer who wants land for his very own, but is willing to accept occupancy and use as the basis of his title, not the right to exploit others.

The correct corollary to the taxation of the rental value of land, as George also pointed out, is the exemption of improvements on the land from taxation. Indeed, I believe in no annual property tax of any sort except on land, and then only for the purpose of abolishing the right of individuals to ground rent. Taxation should fall on income and be proportional to it since it must be paid out of income. (The case for inheritance taxes and a capital levy rests on grounds which I shall discuss later.)

The extraction of mineral wealth involves something very different from the use of land for homes or farms. Mining exhausts the store of the mineral that is mined or the oil that is pumped. There is a sense in which we can speak of the conservation of coal by proper mining, but it is not the same sense in which we can speak of conservation of the soil or the re-creation of forests. Mining and the oil industry cannot possibly be carried on under the process by which a farm family works its farm. They are large-scale industries. They are, moreover, industries in which the key man is not today the promoter or the prospector. He is the geologist or the engineer. Amid all our irrationalities, few things are more absurd than our law that the man who owns the surface of the earth also owns the oil which may be struck a mile below the surface. This theory is responsible for fantastic waste. Men frantically bring in new wells at the very time the operation of old wells is restricted by a legal plan of prorating production. Every owner of the smallest plot in an oil region must hasten to drill his own well or lease his land before "his" oil is exhausted by his neighbor's well.

By logic and experience, therefore, we are driven to propose the following principles in order that the interests of the whole American family, whose heritage is the land, may be saved, and abundance brought forth from it.

1. The title to all mineral wealth should be vested in the government as the agent of society. This fact should be specified in all future deeds to land, and what mineral wealth is now in private hands should be recovered by the government on principles of compensation to be discussed hereafter. Under social ownership of minerals the owner or occupant of the surface of the land shall,

of course, be compensated for loss to him arising from the exercise of the social right to the mineral wealth. The federal government is in far the best position to organize a socially owned coal, iron, copper or oil industry and should be the agent of society rather than of the state governments, but the latter must participate in working out a plan because of their ownership of much land where minerals exist, and their present dependence on the taxation of the land for carrying on education and other functions of local government.

2. Large stands of forests and large acreages of reforested land should be socially owned and socially used, for protection against floods and for supplies of lumber. Federal, state and municipal governments may share in this ownership but should cooperate in a comprehensive plan for the development and use of forests. Woodlots of any considerable size on family farms should be subject to regulation as to use and perpetuation by proper planting.

3. Both city and country lots or acreage should be subject to a tax approximating the rental value of the land apart from improvements on it. The shift to this basis of taxation should be sufficiently gradual to avoid violent financial dislocation, but it should be sure. Society should become the landlord under a system which will permit individuals who so desire to enjoy their own homes and cultivate their own farms and gardens. Henry George's land tax would make this possible while at the same time it would facilitate, rather than impede, great housing developments in cities and cooperative collec-

tives in the country where they are necessary to meet the economic situation. In like manner, the tax would simplify the problems of proper zoning and soil conservation.

THE second essential to an economy of abundance is the proper management of money, or, more specifically, of money, banking and credit. The invention of money was one of man's major achievements. No economy of true abundance is conceivable without it. But like others of his great inventions, man has used money to his own hurt. Properly speaking, money has two functions and only two functions. The first business of money is to facilitate the exchange of goods. The second is to make possible the cost-accounting on which any dynamic society must depend. The trouble is that men have considered money as if in itself it were real wealth, and they have speculated in it on terms which made those who manipulated it masters of the destiny of us all.

Politicians and bankers have been the manipulators. For long periods of time their manipulations were more or less restrained by the quantity of the precious metals used for money; i.e., gold and silver, more particularly gold. Shortage of this monetary supply helped to bring down the Roman Empire. The increase of the supply of precious metals, especially after the conquest of India, helped to finance British capitalism and imperialism in its career of expansion.

Originally there was this much sense in the use of gold and silver: Men extravagantly craved the shiny metals for themselves and what they could make out of them. The metals wore well and could be easily carried. A little of them had therefore great purchasing power. Even in our own day, to the average westerner a silver dollar has a desirable solidity that its paper equivalent lacks. But less and less do silver and gold of themselves have any peculiar value to modern man. By the outbreak of the First World War, gold had monopolized the monetary throne. King Gold ruled as a conveniently accepted fetish. His power depended upon a well-nigh universal make-believe. His dominion tottered under the exigencies of war; it was precariously restored after the war, but his erstwhile devoted subjects, the British, soon dethroned him to their own advantage.

Today in the Second World War the United States is the only great nation even nominally on the gold standard. As a result of an appalling piece of folly, the Roosevelt Administration (with Republican support) wound up its monetary experimentation by agreeing to purchase all the gold offered at $35 an ounce. It has, as a result, 80 per cent of all the gold in the world and is the sole active purchaser. Instead of being a restraint on the inflation to which armament economics tends, this gold is an invitation to it. Messrs. Graham & Whittlesey in their notable book *Golden Avalanche* demonstrate mathematically how this gold may be the basis of astronomical inflation. I agree entirely with their general conclusion that the only possible good in the gold purchase policy is that it is a disguised subsidy to Britain of very great dimensions—and how good that is depends upon one's point of view!

My father was a moralist stern in condemnation of gambling. He made his boys divide up again the marbles they won in a day's games. The only chance that "our" gold will not be a loss or a curse is that we may divide it again with other nations and begin the game over again. And that we are very unlikely to do.

The truth is that today there is no external object of such convenience and universal appeal to men that it can serve as an intrinsic monetary standard. And the spell of gold is so broken that it cannot be restored as a convenient fetish or a medium for settling international balances. The fact that the United States has most of it means that no other nation will be interested in its restoration. All of them will have become used to a managed monetary system. Few forms of propaganda are so viciously misleading as that which suggests that the United States should enter the war in order to guarantee the value of its gold. No military victory will do that, and no gold is worth the cost of war. The sole problem will be to wipe out our losses, born of our own folly, at the price of the least possible financial and political disturbance.

Theoretically I believe in a managed currency directed solely to the maintenance of a stable medium of exchange and cost-accounting. The management should not be by and for private banking interests. Practically, I think Congress and Treasury officials need some protection against manipulative tendencies. I am therefore strongly attracted to the idea of backing the dollar by reserves of actual commodities accumulated according to a weighted index of relative values already worked out by statisticians. The "open market" transactions of the public officials in control could then consist in the necessary purchase and sale of various commodities of use to men in such quantities as might be necessary to stabilize the dollar. Professor Frank Graham of Princeton is one of the economists who is developing this idea.

THE regulation of the value of the dollar is only a part of the problem of money, banking and credit. One of the biggest elements in it is the failure of private investment to provide for expansion in production. Writes Carleton Beals (*Pan America*, p. 248): "Today [before the defense program got under way] utilization of new capital has been hovering around $7,500,000,000—about what it was in 1923. Yet the savings, or surplus profits, from business enterprise was double that during most of the 'twenties." He adds that the discrepancy had grown greater during the 'thirties.

Many sermons with conflicting morals have been preached from the text "Idle Money, Idle Men." To me the soundest are those that teach the necessity of social direction of investment to social ends. Again let us remember that we have far surer knowledge of what we need for human well-being in terms of housing, education, and hospitalization than what we need for adequate military defense. Yet to undertake the former task

144

on any scale comparable to our defense program was deemed impossible for eleven long and bitter years under the old deal and the new.

Those years did bring forth an instrumentality of gigantic possibilities for social control, the brain child not of President Roosevelt, but of President Hoover, the prophet of rugged individualism. I refer, of course, to the Reconstruction Finance Corporation. Under the leadership of Jesse Jones, originally Mr. Hoover's appointee, this agency and its offshoots constitute something more than a gigantic investment bank publicly owned. It is a mammoth credit engine. I quote a summary of its activities from the remarkable account of it by Samuel Lubell in the *Saturday Evening Post* (December 7, 1940):

"So bewildering, startling and colossal an accumulation of financial wonders as Jesse controls probably has never been assembled under one roof before. We can start with what might be called the RFC's portfolio. In it we find the preferred stock of about 4,200 banks, obligations of another 250; the bonds and notes of fifty-four railroads; bonds of more than 1,400 municipalities and other local public bodies: promissory notes of 3,700-plus business firms; almost 50,000 FHA-insured mortgages and another 1,800 real estate mortgages; the capital stock or notes of nine RFC subsidiaries, and obligations of four federal agencies being financed through RFC loans and not congressional appropriations.

"Against its billion and three quarters of outstanding loans and investments, the RFC holds about 1,250,000 items of collateral valued at $2,500,000,000. More than 12,000 separate pieces of property worth nearly $50,-000,000 are owned by the RFC. This is only a corner of the huge foreclosure empire Jones rules. The FHA holds more than $3,000,000 worth of foreclosed homes, and the Home Owners' Loan Corporation holds another 60,000 homes, worth $380,000,000.

"RFC foreclosures, though tiny in comparison, are infinitely richer in variety. Included are a poultry-equipment factory in California, a gold mine in Arizona, a pencil plant in Pennsylvania, a bullfrog-breeding pool in Louisiana; also nine old masters, one a Rubens. Given time, Jesse may yet acquire an RFC art gallery to rival the Frick, Mellon, and Morgan collections.

"Even those collateral and foreclosure figures fail to portray the full sweep of the RFC's financial powers. A single piece of collateral, small in itself, may carry with it control of a veritable empire. In 1935 the RFC came into control of Utilities Power & Light, a company which serves 2,000,000 persons living in nearly 600 communities. Jones sold the stock; another man might have held on to it. Month after month the control of corporations big and small passed through Jesse's big hands."

Mr. Lubell points out how far the RFC has already gone to acquire potential control of banks and railroads to which it has made loans. It has also used its credit to stimulate public ownership of various projects. Already so extensive are Mr. Jones' powers that his sole decision may determine interest rates throughout the country; "by raising or lowering the interest on public money, tremendous subsidies can be siphoned off to any industry." It would be difficult to imagine a more powerful instrumentality of government control, if not government ownership, of all sorts of industries and economic enterprises than already exists in the RFC.

The danger here is that the type of government ownership and control which Mr. Jones is developing will be fascist rather than democratic. Practically, Mr. Jones is now possessed of powers almost as personal and irresponsible as they are vast. Through them the government is acquiring power without first establishing in its own mind, much less in the mind of the public, any real principle for using it.

So far the RFC, itself, has been conducted so as to be solvent with a modest profit. But this has been done only because Jesse Jones has persuaded Congress and the administration to set up separate corporations to finance public lending to foreign countries and to the government relief agencies. These, of course, show anything but a profit. Any transactions of the RFC with these agencies, or in their behalf, or in behalf of political loans to foreign countries, or relief, are treated as outside the sphere of profit and loss. The *Saturday Evening Post* thus comments editorially on this phase of the situation:

"In 1938 his firmament was too full of the red bodies, representing disbursements 'by direction of Congress,' and he asked Congress to wipe out more than $2,500,000,000 of them, which the Congress did. A wiggle of the pen created them; a wiggle of the pen destroyed them. Specifically, the Congress authorized the Secretary of the Treasury to tear up $2,665,000,000 of Jesse

Jones' I O U's and forget them. That was credit the RFC had raised on its notes at the Treasury in order to lend it back to various of the government's own spending agencies. Jesse Jones owed the Treasury, the Treasury owed Jesse Jones, and the Government returned to itself the money it had borrowed from itself, or was it, or did it, or what?"

Unquestionably this editorial comment points to a real danger. It has been very easy for the government to use the RFC and its subsidiaries as "its unknown left hand." But in that policy there are obvious perils to sound financing and to straight thinking about public problems. The correct use of the RFC—and it can be exceedingly effective—requires a clarification of its rôle not only in legislation but in the mind of the public. It should operate for objectives and on principles carefully thought out and laid down. No one man, whatever his ability, should have the power which Jesse Jones now has.

The most efficient use of existing machinery and the most intelligent expansion of our productive capacity do not lie in such indirect control as the RFC is acquiring, but rather in the direct acknowledgment that investment is a social function; that control of banking, more particularly of investment banking, should therefore be social.* Great insurance companies, especially the power-

* Since writing this chapter I have read with great interest the proposals of Adolf A. Berle, Jr., for a capital credit banking system at least partially under public, non-political control. Mr. Berle is thinking constructively in a useful direction. See his chapter on this subject in his recent book, *New Directions in the New World* (Harper's).

ful life insurance companies, come under this head. They control too much capital to be left to their own devices. They have not earned consideration by genuine mutualization or by the most economical service to policy-holders. From the inquiry before the Temporary National Economic Commission I quote almost at random such facts as these:

In 1938, the twenty-six largest life insurance companies had $24,290,000,000 assets. In 1937 the Massachusetts Companies had 54 per cent of lapsed policies, the industrial 64 per cent, against 11 per cent in the state-controlled savings bank insurance plan. Add the cost of agents' commissions and salaries and it is far from a handsome picture.

This does not mean that all banks must be owned by the federal government. Under a sound banking policy there will certainly be place for such democratic agencies as credit unions or cooperative banks and for municipal and state banks, as well as federally owned institutions. The point is that under private banking, investment is exclusively in hope of private profit, and the speculation connected therewith not only gives to private individuals undue power over men, money, and machines, but has failed notably within the last few years to put men, money, and machines to work, as they should have worked for the conquest of poverty. There are too many things which society needs, but which do not seem to promise immediate profit of such magnitude or such security that private capital of its own initiative will enter the field. That is clearly the lesson of the last decade. It is also the lesson taught by the extreme anxiety of private corporations to have the governments, British and American, finance plant expansion for armament purposes. They are afraid of their own ability to utilize enlarged plant capacity for peacetime needs.

THERE is a school of thinkers who believe that increasing government control over credit facilities, plus a broad program of public works, scientific taxation, and possibly some regulation of profits, prices and working conditions, will give us all the social control that we need. I do not accept their conclusions. I think that there are basic enterprises which should immediately be placed under direct social ownership and management. And, contrary to certain critics of socialism, it is precisely because I am sure that such social ownership and management is far more consistent with democracy than the indirect approach. It is true that Germany has achieved astonishing results by state control over economic enterprise rather than by a vast increase of state ownership, but the Nazi government was able to do this because it had first asserted its dictatorial power, claimed from its subjects an implicit obedience, and made them drunk with the terrible wine of an aggressive military patriotism.

In America we want to keep and improve our democracy. It is an unnecessary strain upon that democracy to perpetuate the interest of a large number of absentee owners of enterprises basic to our social life—which interest can always be mobilized politically and industrially in support of the maximum profits. These interests are the natural allies of the political machines which help to keep the masses quiet for them—at a price. When one is dealing with monopoly or semi-monopoly enterprises, it is well to remember the old rule that the hand is quicker than the eye. An administrator with his hand on the job can do things which the regulator catches belatedly if at all. It is by now generally admitted that in the United States publicly owned municipal water systems have made a far better record than privately owned systems under regulation.

Despite extensive propaganda to the contrary by the public utilities, it is evident that Jamestown, New York —to use an example—does a better job by the people in respect to rates and service of electricity than the Consolidated Edison in New York City under public regulation. The beneficiaries of rural electrification have gained far more from direct action by society than from mere regulatory action.

What industries, then, and what services should be socialized? The answers have been many, varied, and all of them suggestive. Thus, society should take over the "basic industries," or, as Lenin once called them, the "commanding heights of industry." Any industry which has been monopolized or semi-monopolized should be taken over by society rather than left to the autocratic power of monopoly in the hands of private individuals. "Let the nation own the trusts" was a good old socialist slogan.

Approaching the matter from a somewhat different

angle, the English economist, John A. Hobson, once suggested that those industries were ripe for socialization in which the initiative of the engineer was more important than the initiative of the enterpriser. If Mr. Hobson were writing today, he might want to expand that suggestion by reason of the fact that enterprises hungry for private profits have lately so conspicuously failed adequately to develop new lines, or to expand the old to meet human needs. Apparently it is engineers *under social direction and for social ends* who must guide the expanding. Nevertheless Mr. Hobson's suggestion has merit.

I should answer the question very much as we answered it in our Socialist platform of 1940.

1. Industries should be monopolized which are very closely connected with the extraction of the mineral wealth, for example, the oil and mining industries. One of the reasons for social ownership in this field is the fact that, to enforce competition, as the government is now trying to enforce it in the oil industry, by legal proceedings, is to encourage waste. Socialization of these industries does not have to follow one uniform pattern. In my judgment there should not be one overall public corporation for coal mining. Certainly there should be one corporation for anthracite and another for soft coal. There might even be regional organization subject to a general plan for the industry.

2. Industry should be socialized in which efficient monopoly organization will best serve the common interest and prevent waste. A good example is in the field of

communication, both by telephone and telegraph. The radio falls into a different category which I shall discuss later. Railroads definitely fall in this field. Competition does not effectively regulate them in the consuming interest, and the present system of regulation of privately owned roads is very cumbersome. There must be one plan for railroads, but the sheer size of the country and of its railroad systems might make it well to organize the railroads in various groups under public corporations, which, with uniformity of working standards and rates, could still have some emulation in service.

There is a special reason for the socialization of railroads. It is that, increasingly, they will have to be operated as a public service. The day when they can be great moneymakers is gone. A third of them are, or have recently been, bankrupt, and another third are still trembling on the brink—partly as a result of their past sins, partly by reason of changing conditions. Railroading is decidedly an industry in which the desire for private profit, given the history and present condition of railroads, does not minister to service. In the emergency of the First World War, it was necessary for the government to take them over. It did this on terms which unscientifically guaranteed profits to the owners, and there has been a vast deal of propaganda to the effect that government operation was inefficient and costly. This propaganda is rejected by the almost unanimous opinion of the real experts in the field. In recent years it is significant that such improvements as there have been in a very backward passenger service on the railroads have come as a result of public prodding, not private initiative, and they have been financed almost entirely by RFC loans.

3. Industries and services should be socialized whenever and wherever private monopoly, the approach to private monopoly, or the agreement between large-scale corporations, restricts production to less than is justified by the social usefulness of the product. The steel and cement industries are outstanding examples in this field. Another example, of a somewhat different sort, is to be found in the processing and distribution of milk. Two gigantic corporations or holding companies, the National Dairy Products Company and Borden's, virtually monopolize the field. Their structure is made to order to conceal profits. In New York State, at one and the same time, children of the city get less milk than is necessary for a maximum standard of health, largely because their parents can't afford it, and the farmers who produce the milk can rarely meet the depreciation charges on their capital equipment. Regulation is, at best, ineffective. There has never been a proper investigation of hidden profits in the processing and delivery of milk. What apparent competition there is tends to raise prices, because of the wasteful methods of distribution. The situation cries aloud for a solution by public corporations or by a combination of farmers' and consumers' cooperatives, or by a mixture of both of them.

There are two other principles of socialization which somewhat overlap those which I have laid down.

The first of these is that industries and services should

be socialized whenever and wherever the concentration of economic power creates a political interest which is too strong for a democracy to tolerate in private hands. In recent years this principle would apply particularly to the power industry, which is basic in modern civilization. On every account it should be socialized. Insofar as there is competition today it tends to be wasteful, and to hinder the best possible coordination of service. In years gone by this industry has been particularly culpable in its deliberate effort to prostitute democracy by its propaganda and its lobbying tactics. It is not enough to try to break up unnatural holding companies, or to erect yardsticks, excellent as some of them may be. What is needed is a comprehensive plan; the basic principle of that plan might well be that large centers for generating power, by the use of either water or steam, and high power lines connecting them and servicing municipalities and districts, should be federally owned. Electric power districts and municipalities should create public corporations for the distribution of power and encourage cooperatives. Present plans of rural electrification should be utilized and where municipal power plants are operating efficiently they should be fitted in to the general system.

Our second and final principle is operative in many fields: whenever and wherever ownership has lost its management function, profits cannot be construed as, in any way, the wages of management. If the business is directed by hired men, these hired men, technicians, engineers and the like, should be working for public, not private, owners.

It will be observed that these principles do not contemplate a static, once-and-for-all determination of what industries and services should pass into the hands of public corporations, and be managed for the general advantage rather than the profits of private owners. But neither do these principles contemplate a whimsical and capricious policy which will leave the enterprises no sense of security. Their proper interpretation and application might clear the air and permit an actual simplification of some of the unscientific and bureaucratic types of taxation and regulation under which private enterprise now suffers.

We contemplate a large area of action in which, subject to regulations in the interest of the workers, both as producers and consumers, private ownership and management may be effective, and profiteering prevented by the right sort of taxation, and the preservation of a genuine competition. Even in this field it may be necessary for the government to set up yardstick enterprises occasionally, as a check to what is going on. And if private enterprise is as slow as it has been these last years in undertaking new enterprises, it will be necessary to establish public corporations to do what private owners cannot or will not do. Already in the field of housing it has become a certainty that only public corporations can produce low-cost housing.

SINCE chronic unemployment on an immense scale is proof of the necessity of a new order and of democratic socialization, that new order must expect to be judged by its success in abolishing such unemployment. It can be done by a deliberate purpose to produce what is needed, and by direction of social savings and credit to that end. I have already indicated that an elastic public works program is not only valuable in itself as creating social income, but in taking up such slack as may occur from time to time in the process of adjustment of economic enterprises. Besides a PWA program, we shall probably have to continue some sort of equivalent to our present WPA program, and supplement unemployment insurance by giving socially useful work to men and women temporarily out of employment during readjustment. But that WPA program ought to be small and of a genuinely emergency sort, dealing with hundreds of thousands and not with millions. One of the purposes of the social direction of industrial expansion is to see that every American can expect useful work under normal conditions.

An important factor in bringing about such continuous employment will be a reduction of hours with a consequent increase in the number of workers, but to make the main hope of the abolition of unemployment an ironbound reduction of hours would be dangerous. It would tend to give us a sharing of poverty, not abundance. The Brookings Institution and other authorities have proved statistically that by no means can the nation as yet produce what the nation wants and needs on the basis of a binding 30-hour week in all industries.

The program which I have outlined will make possible an enormous increase in the national income, but there is no plan so perfect and no state so wise and good that the people can put all their trust in a program and a government. In many fields, as I have already indicated, a consumers' cooperative may be preferable to a publicly-owned corporation or supplemental to it, or even a friendly competitor of it with advantage to society. Something of the sort can be observed in successful action in Sweden, at least in Sweden before it fell under the shadow of Nazi power. I do not think we are in position today to lay down a precise formula for dividing the field between public corporations and cooperatives. Much depends upon the rapidity of a healthy growth of the latter. Public corporations are preferable for dealing with natural monopoly or situations in which there can be no voluntary element in the cooperation of the consumers of a product, or users of a service.

Labor unions we shall continue to need so long as there is a difference of interest between those who invest their labor in a specific task and those who consume its product. As the class division between an owning class and the mass of workers is abolished or greatly minimized by the successful working of our program, the function of the labor union as the competent day-by-day organization for such struggle should be reduced to a vanishing point. To be successful, the union will have to be progressively interested in the productive process —a thing which fortunately seems to be happening already in some of the more advanced sections of the needle trades. Walter Reuther's proposal for the utilization of waste space in the automotive industry for airplane production and Philip Murray's proposals for labor participation in production councils were encouraging illustrations of this attitude. Nevertheless in a dynamic democratic economy the existence of labor unions as the spokesmen for the special interest of workers in particular enterprises and, even to a degree, as bargainers for those interests, should be preserved. What the new order cannot tolerate is the exclusive union which sets up a job monopoly. Its doors must be open to all workers in the industry in which it functions. The excuse for a job monopoly under private capitalism will have disappeared under an order whose business will be to achieve jobs for all. This can certainly be done by guidance without conscription, but no man and no organized group can say: "We will work only at this one trade or calling or else we won't work at all."

Strikes ought to be unnecessary under the program we are trying to work out. They may constitute a very unsocial instrument in the hands of labor—for instance, the strike of a comparatively small number of employees in a key industry like the production of power, could conceivably tyrannize a whole community. Nevertheless, the best way to deal with potential dangers of strikes is to provide substitute methods of adjusting such conflicts in interest as will perist under any society. Those who do not like the totalitarian state need to beware about glib acceptance of the formula, "You can't strike against the government," which Mr. Roosevelt has used. That might easily lead to totalitarian control of organized labor as in Russia or the fascist countries, since more and more industries will be owned or controlled by the government. Ethically more significant considerations bearing on the right to strike are to be found in the nature of the enterprise itself, the effect of a strike in it upon the community, and above all, in the substitutes offered to the workers in their struggle for better conditions. For it must be remembered that strikes or the right to strike are vital in labor's progress. At their worst they have involved no such violence and hurt to the common weal as the methods of riot and war by which political issues have been fought out.

So FAR we have been discussing steps necessary for the increase of production to something like the maximum of our technological capacity. Only indirectly have we dealt with the problem of distribution of what is produced. Yet increased production not only will be impossible, but, if it were possible, would be of little social value, were the distribution of the national income to be so grotesquely and outrageously unjust as it is at the present time. It is simply impossible for anyone to prove that the present range of income in America from less than $300 to more than $1,000,000 a year corresponds to any principle of justice or common sense. From scores of platforms in the last ten years I have challenged audiences to list the 50, or 400 or 500, largest incomes in America and to tell what their recipients have done to earn so much. In a great many cases, the answer would be "they have done us"—legally, under our present standard, of inheritance and absentee ownership, but unethically.

As a philosophical policeman once said to me, after he had been obliged to arrest me in a free speech test case, "Mr. Thomas, what you was doing was moral all right, even if it ain't legal. Some things is legal that ain't moral and some things is moral that ain't legal, and what's a poor cop going to do about it?" Let us consider what the public ought to do about it.

Even the more conservative among us might be surprised if suddenly they should realize the scale on which they are now accepting as a matter of course the principle that much of our income should be social; that is to say, exist in such form that it can be used and enjoyed by whoever will. It is a rôle played in modern life by parks, playgrounds, highways, museums, public educational facilities, concerts, down through a list too long to enumerate. Even our health, in a country which has by no means formally adopted any type of "socialized medicine," is largely dependent upon public health activity. One of the principles of distribution in the good society will be a great increase in the rôle of the social income.

But never will the need of adequate individual income for any full and gracious life disappear. Men will never be content that they and their children should be housed and fed on the principle of life in army barracks. Public libraries will never, altogether, satisfy the wants of the men who love books, nor public concerts the musicians' need for their own instruments. There is a great variety of consumers' goods which enrich life and which, to be enjoyed, require individual ownership. We want more, not less, of this kind of private property, the possession of which need exploit no other men in the world.

To satisfy the necessity for individual income, some principle of remuneration must be established. Ethically the loftiest of all the principles which have been advanced is the familiar socialist slogan, "from every man according to his ability, to every man according to his need." The Communists will still tell you that communism will be achieved when that principle is carried out. (Stalin, however, is in no hurry, to establish it in his domain.)

Noble as is this principle, it is scarcely an adequate guide in practical economics to the apportionment of income. On what external basis is *need* to be determined? Or, for that matter, *ability*? Not only in our own day, but for many a long day to come, this slogan will probably be an ideal or leavening influence rather than a practical principle of remuneration.

Another principle of remuneration is expressed by another formula, popular among socialists and other workers: "To every worker the social value of his toil." Here, also, there are difficulties. In a simpler society it would be easier to approximate a fairly accurate judgment as to what a given man produces and as to its social value. In this day of specialization, of men on the assembly line, white-collar workers, engineers, and so on, the task is much harder. Who shall judge the precise product or social value of the toil of such representative workers as a policeman, street cleaner, salesman, engineer, skilled tool maker and a beginner on the assembly line? Some socialists, among them Bernard Shaw, have argued for equality of payment. Shaw partially refutes his own argument by proposing shorter hours with the same pay for a peculiarly hard or exhausting job. The difficulty with this principle in the present state of social development is very practical. There are just two ways in which we can get men to undertake, on the one hand, unpleasant jobs and, on the other hand, jobs requiring unusual types of ability and skill. The first way is by coercion or conscription; either coercion by lack of opportunity with which we are familiar today, or the conscription of the state. The second is to attract them by differential rewards.

In saying this, I am by no means affirming that the sole incentives to work are bitter necessity and differential material rewards. On the contrary, one of our hopes for a new order is the fact that today men so obviously work for the satisfaction of creating and for the joy of mutual aid. Nevertheless these incentives to excellent work can scarcely be reckoned in arranging a wage and salary schedule. It is certainly better for society and the individual to obtain service by extra reward for unpleasant work—which, to be sure, is not the present custom— or for jobs requiring unusual skill—which to some extent is our present custom—than to resort to conscription of labor.

Our best immediate plan of distributing the national income will be based on a combination of two principles:

a basic payment to a man or, better, to a family, on the basis of a common need, a kind of social dividend * accruing to the individual from his membership in the productive unit which is society. Above that, a payment according to deed, roughly calculated, to be sure, on the basis of existing customs rather than an accurate measure of social value, but nevertheless designed to stimulate essential work. The scale, of course, should be subject to revision and improvement.

In the problem of working out the distribution of an increasing national income by a combination of the principles of reward according to need and deed, we have to help us, under the plan we have proposed, increased knowledge of what the circumstances of our people really are, and a sharp and increasing diminution of the economic and political power of an owning class to take toll from wealth as they will, regardless of the services they may render. The tools of more equitable distribution are already in use in the world. They include the power to tax, the right of labor unions to bargain collectively, legislative provision for minimum wages and maximum hours, care always being taken that such provisions constitute a ceiling for hours and a floor for wages, and not a straitjacket for both. Outside of these provisions for proper payment of labor, there must be steady improvement in provisions for workmen's compensation in case of accident and occupational diseases; and for unemployment insurance, supplemented by

* I am indebted to Major Douglas for the phrase although I do not accept his system as a whole.

public work for those who may be temporarily unemployed for a shorter or longer period.

Society, as we have said, also has a responsibility for its children and for its older members—this on the principle of society as a family, as well as, if one prefers, the great productive unit. The present interest of the community is in old age pensions and allowances, and some of the impossible demands made by the advocates of specific plans must not be allowed to obscure the validity of more moderate claims. I am in favor of a universal old age payment at sixty or sixty-five. It would probably be better and cheaper to administer such a plan than to invoke income tests. Then we can depend upon proper taxation to take care of the situation under which some would have too much.

Proper upbringing of our children is even more important than old age allowances. Especially at a time when there is a declining birth rate there is a strong case for the principle of family allowances for which I once argued, but on which I have said little lately because other types of social benefits have been more in the public consciousness. Family allowances should be granted under certain restrictions, or with certain accompaniments, of which perhaps the most important is the orderly and legalized dissemination by competent physicians of information about birth control. It is already desirable in many sections of the population to stimulate more births.

It would be unwise, I think, to try to fix by law an absolute maximum or minimum individual or family income. The maximum can be taken care of by taxation; the minimum should be approximated deliberately and by plan in the light of our steadily increasing statistical knowledge of the level made possible by our technological progress. At the present time Dr. Mordecai Ezekiel and other competent economists, as we have seen, assure us that we have the productive capacity to make $2,500 a minimum annual family income. Both wage provisions and provisions concerning the social dividend should then be administered with a view to making that minimum income the portion of every American family worth holding together at all. Those families in which fathers or mothers, or both, are so completely shiftless and irresponsible that even state custodial care of children is better than theirs should be broken up. Such families will be found far fewer in number than ever in human history when the burden of want and worry is lifted, even to the extent that a $2,500 minimum would make possible.

ONE of the most important aspects of the use of the national income concerns the preservation and increase of public health. As medicine becomes more informed of the nature and prevention of diseases, it must of necessity become more and more specialized. Often the diagnosis requires a whole congress of physicians and surgeons to gather around one patient and to stake out their respective claims. Only a few of the rich can pay the legitimate charges for such service. In addition, therefore, to what is now accepted as a matter of course in the way of public health service, there must and will be some form, or perhaps several supplementary forms, of socialized medicine. I am no expert in this field, nor shall I hold back this book till I have become one. I should like a system which would permit us to have one physician to whom we can go, much as our fathers went to the family doctors, for general advice and reference to specialists.

Voluntary cooperation has already shown what can be done to pay for hospitalization, and to aid men and women of moderate incomes to preserve their own and their children's health. I should be inclined to favor an extension of this principle, plus far more ample provision of hospitals and clinics, with salaried physicians, to a bureaucratic system of medical insurance. We have a right to ask some of these able physicians who spend much time in a hopeless fight against socialized medicine, to apply their particular knowledge in the field to guiding us to the best form of it.

In all this outline of an economic order of abundance, taxation has run as a recurrent theme. It is so important that it must be examined by itself. There are some principles which should be laid down:

1. Taxation should be according to ability to pay, that is, it should fall primarily upon income not on static wealth. Sales taxes which do fall on incomes are unjust to individuals and economically retrogressive because of their reduction of purchasing power of those consumers who most need to purchase more. The Northwestern

Life Insurance Company has shown that a man with a wife and two children who earns $80 a month pays 12.99 per cent in hidden taxes. The *New York Sun*, with no desire to demand more progressive taxes, on January 11, 1941, made the following statement:

"In the year 1932, the wage earners, salaried workers, professional men and home makers, representing about 95 per cent of the people, paid just less than 60 per cent of the local tax burden. But by 1939 this tax burden jumped up to at least 77 per cent of the actual tax collections in addition to which were the huge federal deficits which must be paid sometime in taxes. For the year 1940, because of the cost of national defense, the share of the classes mentioned will be somewhere between 90 and 95 per cent."

For all this mass of hidden taxation on income, bearing disproportionately on low income groups, properly graduated income taxes must be substituted. There should be no tax-exempt bonds, and income of, and from, socialized industries should be subject to taxation. Especial effort should be made to recover war or armament profits by taxation.

2. Taxation should be as simple as possible, as uncomplicated, as definite, and as easily understood as human skill can make it. There is no rational excuse for our present American chaos in taxes. There are 126 hidden or indirect taxes on one single pair of shoes. States are setting up virtual tariffs on their borders. The internal free trade which has so greatly promoted American prosperity is being wiped out under various pre-

texts by taxes on trucks crossing state lines and a dozen other devices. That should be stopped. The number of independent taxing agencies should be reduced to a minimum—there are, I believe, more than 100 such bodies in Cook County, Illinois. Various government authorities may report what they think they need but there should be a comprehensive federal, state, and local budget, and a comprehensive tax. Indeed, I should like to see a plan worked out which would result in one income tax divided between the federal and state governments.

3. There are special reasons for three forms of taxation: (a) The tax on the rental value of land which we have already discussed. (b) Inheritance taxes. It is the living, not the dead, who create wealth. It usually hurts, not helps, the individual to exempt him from the common lot of toil because of his careful selection of his ancestors. Above a very moderate minimum, inheritance taxes should approximate 100 per cent. The manner and time of their collection, however, should extend special consideration to widows and children under age. Their terms should make it relatively easy for homes and farms—not great estates—to stay in the same families from generation to generation, if their possessors so desire. Moreover, I think that it should be made easier rather than harder for families to keep personal possessions, furniture, books and pictures as heirlooms. (c) In two Presidential campaigns, 1932 and 1936, I laid stress on the idea of a carefully graduated capital levy with a double purpose in view: First, the reduction

of the national indebtedness; and second, active aid to the process of socialization. I laid less stress upon this tax in 1940 because of the pressure of other issues. I am still of the opinion that the day will come when such a capital levy as I am proposing will be an invaluable factor in any alternative to wild ruin or wholesale expropriation; to astronomical inflation, or to the paralysis of society under the weight of debt and retrogressive taxes.

I also think that this tax may supply a valuable part of the answer to the much discussed question of *compensation*. Socialists have long been familiar with the inevitable question: "By what process do you expect to acquire under democratic socialization the property you now wish to socialize?" Their answers have been varied. My own would run about as follows: Of the different types of private property, those have the least basis in ethics or in sound economics which entitle the alleged owner, usually the absentee owner of stocks or bonds or lands, to an inescapable claim upon the lives and labors of his fellows. Nevertheless, confiscation is an idea which in human experience has been associated with gross tyranny and grave social disorder. The very word evokes fear in the little man who still thinks he has something to lose by it, no matter how much he may envy the rich. Moreover, unless society is in a position to take over all productive property at once and make it work—and our society is not ready to do this—there is no equity in expropriating without compensation stockholders of the steel trust but not the owners of beauty parlors or printing plants which would not be taken over. The principle of compensation is therefore pragmatically valuable for peaceful and orderly change—an inducement to facilitate such change, rather than to block it by violence or sabotage. So great is the productive capacity of our modern industrial apparatus that if it is kept going ever more efficiently it can rapidly meet almost any claim against it better than the disrupting paralysis of it.

Obviously, however, compensation must not indefinitely perpetuate a social class of owners, and it must not leave those owners in a position of power over the socialized industry. Society must be hard-boiled in computing the compensation. It can and should develop lands and mineral wealth that already belong to it or have reverted to it, rather than pay fantastic prices for privately owned property. The equity of bank stockholders when the government intervened to save the banks in 1933 was very small indeed. Today a reasonable price for the purchase of the railroads of the United States, based, let us say, on what their securities are worth in a capitalist market, would be far less than the owners are likely to ask.

Bearing these things in mind, the government might follow one of two courses: The first, to which on the whole I am inclined, would be the purchase of all or most of the enterprises to be socialized at prices within the bounds of reason; payment to be made in bonds of the socialized industry to be amortized within, let us say, twenty years. The carrying charges would be far less than those which industry bears today. The alternative sometimes urged is an annuity of limited term for those whose property is taken.

In any case, compensation should be accompanied, in my judgment, by a graduated capital levy assessed upon wealth from whatever source it might be derived. The principle would at one and the same time reduce the cost of acquiring certain properties, and equalize the treatment of property holders on the basis of the tax paid. The most important of its advantages, however, would be the fact that the levy would prevent such wholesale and promiscuous confiscation as great inflation or economic paralysis has always imposed. If, because of the hardness of men's hearts or the sluggishness of their imagination, socialization must come out of war, violent revolution, or complete economic collapse, it is certain it will not offer compensation to anyone. Yet everyone will pay a tremendous price beyond anything that even exaggerated compensation would impose. Remember the cost of the Civil War as compared with what the cost would have been for abolishing chattel slavery by compensation.

IN THIS rough sketch of a bridge for the future there is one obvious omission. We have not discussed the problem of agriculture except in passing reference to land ownership. Yet the production of foodstuffs is the most basic of all human callings. Agriculture in the United States today suffers from two difficulties which no social program, however excellent, can ignore or easily overcome.

First, American agriculture is pretty steadily losing its world market under the pressure of various nationalistic systems. For certain of our crops which were among the most important of our exports in former years, notably cotton and wheat, I see no recovery to anything like their former importance, even if nationalistic economics after the war abates more than I think probable. The culture of wheat, cotton, and other crops will be intensified wherever it has been established. For one reason, prices adequate to sustain what we like now to call the "American standard of living" will be hard to pay. For another reason, it seems probable that even with a return to fairly normal conditions, the decline in the birth rate, now so important a phenomenon in Western Europe and the United States, will become more general, so that there will be no longer an increase in the numbers who must be fed if they are to live. American agriculture was prosperous when that increase, combined with a rising standard of living, ran along with or ahead of increased production by the use of new lands and improved tools and methods.

It is this matter of improvement which constitutes the second great problem of agriculture. The machine age came late to the farmer but it has come hard. It isn't merely that modern machinery and positive knowledge of the soil permit the farmer to grow more, it is also that he must meet the competition of synthetic textiles and even, to some extent, synthetic food: the products of the laboratory and the factory. There are already signs that a man with skill, water, and some chemicals can raise more vegetables in tanks than on acres of land.

A sympathetic writer, Charles Morrow Wilson, in his recent book *Corn Bread and Creek Water* calls present-day farming "the most madly extravagant of all our great enterprises." According to his compilation of figures, the average yield of wheat is 15 bushels an acre against a possible 122; cotton, one-third of a bale as against a possible 3⅓ bales; potatoes, 115 bushels as against 1,055. Which is one reason why reduction of acreage does not necessarily mean reduction of crops. The thrifty farmer may use payments for planting fewer acres to fertilize the others and raise more. Consumers need more vegetables but Mr. Wilson tells us that 2.8 tons of vegetable materials have to be raised yearly in order to provide each average one of us with 1.4 tons to eat! And O. P. Wilcox in an earlier book, *Reshaping Agriculture*, says that under the best farming practice it would be comparatively easy to eliminate four out of five acres from cultivation, and four out of five farmers, and feed America well.

The return to the soil is no solution for our economic problems; it promises no economy of abundance. The relative increase of rural population in the 'thirties was a sign of the sickness, not the health, of our nation. The day of the great cities as Frank Lloyd Wright, and others have hoped, may be ending. Production may be decentralized. An increasing number of people may delight in their own lawns and gardens. But agriculture, as an occupation, cannot healthfully absorb the unemployed; it must count on sending many of its own sons into the ever expanding mechanical industries to satisfy man's well-nigh limitless wants and needs.

Nevertheless, it is by no means true, as yet, that American farmers suffer because the American people are already too well fed and too well clothed. The contrary is the case. The children of the growers of our cotton rarely have underclothes. In the South, the growers of our food have themselves an inadequate and badly balanced diet. The people of America, as a whole, need more of almost every major food product except wheat—and possibly barley and rice—in order to be well fed. It follows that the primary emphasis on agricultural recovery depends upon raising the general standards and purchasing power of the American people. The answer to the problem of the country is in the town.

While agriculture is definitely in a transitional period, it should be so treated. It is not fair for the farmers to bear all the cost of readjustment, especially since they have no ability to protect themselves equivalent to that of the industrialists or even the organized workers.

From that point of view, the administration's present policy of aid to agriculture is justified in broad outline. I think the food-stamp plan has especial merit. Agricultural relief fails because it has not been accompanied by a sufficiently vigorous or adequate program for bringing to us a general economy of abundance. It is open to criticism because it has paid too much attention to limitation of crops and maintenance of price and too little attention to the restoration of our badly exhausted soil. Simultaneously we have been paying farmers not to produce on land well watered by the rain, while we have been spending other millions to bring desert land under cultivation by irrigation. There has not been a proper correlation of policy.

Finally, the administration's present policy, especially in the plantation country, helps the owners rather than the tenants, sharecroppers, and field hands. Senator Bilbo of Mississippi once casually admitted at a Senatorial hearing on the demand of southern sharecroppers for certain minimum guaranties, that two landowners in his county received more than 80 per cent of all the benefit payments by the government.

Plantation owners, themselves rarely very rich today, permit extraordinarily little to reach their tenants and field hands. At very least, no benefits should be paid to landlords except on condition of their honoring certain minimum standards set up in contracts with tenants and sharecroppers, and by agreement with field hands on wages and hours. But the plantation system as a whole should be abolished. We do not have to solve once and for all the question of cooperatives or collectives versus family farms. We can leave that to a natural evolution, always provided that we encourage cooperation among farmers, especially in the field of marketing, and that by governmental power we substitute cooperative collectives for great plantations, and for the factories in the fields now owned by private individuals.

It is quite evident that this outline plan for industry, agriculture or both requires a certain degree of planning.

By no means does it require the kind of regimentation that Russia has been practising, or the arbitrary control which has imposed a military economy on Germany, and will probably impose it on our own nation under the necessities of our chaotic defense program, even if we escape war. I challenge any thoughtful reader to show any logical necessity why the program we have been discussing requires, as is so often alleged, a totalitarian dictatorship.

Again let me remind students of technical economics that the contention of Von Mises and his disciples—that under anything short of laissez-faire, cost-accounting and the price system necessary to dynamic economics break down—has been refuted in theoretical terms by the work of Oskar Lange, and other socialist economists. It is refuted by the experience both of Russia and Germany. Whatever their faults, their economy, including military production, has been expanding, not contracting. In Russia it might have expanded faster but for the mistakes of over-regimentation and the compulsory collectivization of agriculture. Indeed, planning in the end will be frustrated, not helped, by dictatorship. Prohibition of self-criticism will mean an inescapable dry rot.

The principal element in planning the program we have been considering is the direction of investment and of production by a general socialization of the credit system. We shall definitely need a National Planning Council, and probably regional councils (subject to broad determination of policies by the legislature, but divorced from immediate political control) to coordinate and interpret statistics and economic trends, and to produce a balanced program of expansion. They will use the price mechanism and cost-accounting to guide them, but they, more especially the national council, must have definite powers of decision. It is largely the failure of the price system to function automatically in providing abundance which calls planning boards into existence. Planning in the United States will be easier because we are less dependent than most nations on foreign trade and hence can better direct our destiny. Foreign trade, whether we like it or not, will almost certainly have to be managed more closely after the war than ever before, no matter who may win.

The actual control over industry by planning councils can be, I suspect, far less drastic than the War Industries Board set up in the First World War or than OPM will establish in our present gigantic defense enterprise. It will essentially be a more normal program since it will emphasize production for human need, and not for that waste which armament economics is.

Those who fear that such planning councils as I am suggesting will be nothing but a further addition to an already weighted bureaucracy are in error. A normally functioning, expanding economic system properly guided can dispense with a lot of red tape and the regulatory machinery of bureaucracies whose business is not to do something, but to watch somebody else do it.*

In the interest of freedom from the wrong sort of

* The best single book I know on this subject is Barbara Wootton's *Plan or No Plan* (Farrar and Rinehart).

political control, it might be well to establish the principle that planning councils should be chosen from panels suggested to the President, by associations of engineers and technicians, farmers, producers and consumers.

The workers themselves should be protected by an improved system of civil service. That system should not on the one hand exclude the right to join their own unions or on the other protect inefficiency. With time and patience a way can be found to prevent the exploitation of civil service employees or their organization into a horde of mercenaries by certain political leaders without depriving them of the ordinary rights of citizens to the extent threatened by the Hatch Act.

The real danger of dictatorship arises not from any logical impossibility of democracy's establishment of orderly and effective social control, but rather from the apathy of citizens except in time of great emotional excitement, and their tendency to put all their trust in a leader. There is no way of saving democracy from the people themselves and their own blunders. There are ways, however, of simplifying the processes of democracy, making it seem more interesting and important, of introducing functional democracy, and clarifying issues. We can teach ourselves and our children from the cradle to the grave to look upon the state not as our god and master but as our powerful servant for the good not so much of an abstract class or mass as of all of us as individuals. This theory of the state requires a guaranty of certain rights of individuals beyond the reach not only of the mob or the bureaucrats but also of political majori-

179

ties. A lively sense of the importance of our civil liberties and a capacity to apply them under changing circumstances is the necessary condition of the good society of the future.

In the business of making democracy work there is a homely but very practical matter which is too often overlooked. The spirit of democracy must be carried into unions, cooperatives, civic societies, etc., and liberty of discussion must be preserved in them if it is to be valued in the government of the state. But sad experience teaches us that our workaday democracy in these organizations as well as in our legislatures is a time-wasting business. If I did my full duty by my party, my union, my cooperative, I should have no time to live—or make a living. And much of this "duty" is waste motion which repels all but those of a certain temperament who love wrangling and protracted debate. Those who can wear down a democratic body by sheer endurance have not necessarily the best temperament for effective action. Better techniques of democracy must be found for quick disposal of unimportant issues and for setting the time of voting on important issues; there must be a better use of committees or sub-committees to save time and energy of the whole group.

To RETURN to governmental matters: I am wholly opposed to exclusive government ownership or control of the press, motion pictures, and radio. And it is precisely this control which comes easiest to governments. The government may legitimately or even usefully employ existing machinery to spread information about matters which concern us as citizens. There is a place for official publicity. Moreover, it would be a good thing if a minimum but adequate amount of political argumentation on different sides of issues presented in political campaigns should be put before the voters at public expense. This should be accompanied by more effective limitations on private expenditures by wealthy parties than now exist. But the government should never be allowed to monopolize the press, radio, or motion picture industry, or to regiment them as they are regimented in totalitarian countries.

The problem of financing privately owned radio stations and newspapers will have to be worked out along new lines as the volume of competitive commercial advertising diminishes. (That will not be an unmixed evil!) But the increase in the income of most of us will permit us to finance such enterprises if we will.

We can also finance to some extent educational projects which may challenge an unwholesome governmental monopoly in this field. But education from the kindergarten to the university will have to be, as it already is, in the main a charge on the national or state budget, determined along with other social charges, and administered in accordance with the principles of academic freedom essential to good teaching. Since the resources of our 48 states are so unequal, there must be a federal subsidy to the public schools, granted on condition of an end of discrimination against colored children and colored schools in the South.

When changing economic institutions make it impossible for useful private universities to live off endowments, society may well consider grants to them, provided that their friends at least partially support them, and, in return for public help, impose no religious or political tests on students or faculty.

So WE come to the end of a long and, I fear, dull outline of what ought to be the most exciting subject in the world: the conquest of poverty without war or dictatorship. From my outline there have been some obvious omissions to which we shall turn in the next chapter. But first we must consider briefly the most obvious of them all, and that is direct treatment of the bearing of our costly defense program on this plan.

I have deliberately ignored it in this chapter save for passing reference because I wished to show what might be done in a nation primarily concerned for the war against poverty. Had we sooner begun action along these lines we might even have made the financing of an expensive program of military defense a by-product of gearing our machinery to abundance; we shall not, I repeat, make abundance a by-product of gearing our machinery to war or defense on the scale that is now probable. Under the wisest plan we shall have to pay for defense by sacrificing a large measure of material well-being. But even partial effort to get butter as well as guns, while keeping freedom; even a secondary attention to fiscal problems and true social security, will bring rewards. There is a difference between more and less bad. And to get the less bad, I should be willing to hitch a positive good like the abolition of slums to a "defense" program although that approach, rather than a direct appeal to human values, grinds my spirit!

There will come a time when the center of interest for us, and possibly the world, will shift to economic conditions, all too likely to economic crisis. The greater the crisis and the hysteria which will accompany it, the worse for this orderly plan we have examined. But if we can keep out of belligerent participation in this war, we may have time, facilities, and the attitude necessary for orderly solution of our problems. Even if we are caught in war, it is a necessity of life to believe that in happier days men who have not ceased to hope and plan may yet build a society free from insecurity, poverty and exploitation. If the worst befalls, to keep alive faith in the possibility of a rational plan for harnessing machinery to life and abundance is a service to ourselves, to our children, and their children who must take up the unfinished task. It is a task which never can be ended until at last men prepare arms against no enemy except poverty, natural disaster, and disease. When they will plan for this great end, they cannot fail. It is an immediate service, *now*, to emphasize that fact and to illustrate in some detail what might be done about it.

CHAPTER VIII ☆ UNFINISHED BUSINESS

A TITLE such as I have given this chapter demands explanation. Perhaps, the reader will add, apology. A design for the future is of necessity unfinished; for that matter, life, itself, is unfinished business. But, in a peculiar sense, I find myself thinking of certain problems as unfinished. And I group them together under that rather subjective classification, instead of trying to fit them into a more logical pattern. In short, in this chapter, I am talking about some of the problems I find hardest to answer even by way of suggestive outline.

The first of these problems concerns the adequacy of our governmental structure to the conduct of the good society. Under our Constitutional theory and practice, we have enjoyed obvious advantages; certain elemental rights of individuals have been given protection as against the power of the majority or the government of the state itself. Imperfect as that protection has often been, in these days of totalitarian states it is a very precious thing. And next, the federal principle not only made possible union of the thirteen original states, but the rapid development of a whole continent without excessive centralization. Finally, we have developed capacities of government, of political action and, on the whole, a power of executive leadership falling short of dictatorship, as the parliamentary governments of the great nations of continental Europe did not.

But against these advantages there are certain structural defects which not only would make difficult the carrying out of such a plan as I have suggested for reorganizing our economic life, but which menace the smooth working of the government we have. The god who is said to care for fools and drunkards must have an especial affection for America.

Until recently, in reciting a list of these defects, I put first government by the Supreme Court. I shall not now repeat my indictment, so profoundly has the Court changed its attitude and its line of decisions since it gave validity to the Wagner Labor Relations Act. I shall only repeat a conclusion for which I have elsewhere argued at length. The Supreme Court has value, constitutionally, because it affords a means of settling disputes between states and even between state and federal power. It has, or may have, even greater value under our American way of life and thought as a protector of civil liberty. But its power was a positive danger when the judges read Herbert Spencer, or some other thinker of the nineteenth century, into the Constitution, and in the light of their prejudices really wrote not only their own law, but rewrote the Constitution itself as if they were a permanent Constitutional Convention. Under the line taken by the Court as reconstituted under the Roosevelt Administration, this danger has been greatly mitigated, if it has not passed altogether. An amendment to the Constitution limiting the power of the Court is therefore by no means as necessary as it seemed to me when I wrote *After the New Deal, What?* as recently as 1936. The thing that I chiefly fear from the present Court is the establishment of a kind of religion of state if it follows the precedent set in its eight-to-one decision against the Witnesses for Jehovah.

At present the greatest danger in our Constitutional system is of deadlock when action is imperative. The Constitution itself, and accepted custom, have brought it to pass that that danger does not exist in time of war (when we have more reason to fear that the President will become too much of a dictator) but in peace times a quarreling President and Congress can tie up the country. It would not even take a united Congress. Either the House or the Senate might do the job.

Actually this paralysis of effective government has not occurred to as serious an extent as one might have expected. For many periods of our national life we could get along pretty well even if the national government did not act aggressively. Weak Presidents usually yielded to Congress; strong Presidents for a considerable period of time have mastered Congress, but not by ways conducive to the health of democracy. They have felt compelled to make an effective use of patronage; they have gone to the people—not as in England, through a general election—with a demand that public opinion club Congress into line. In recent critical years, the President has extorted from Congress itself emergency powers of vast and ill-defined extent. The lack of any Constitutional machinery in America for preventing the deadlock of which I speak gravely increases the danger of irresponsible dictatorship as the alternative to paralysis.

Woodrow Wilson, as a college professor, used to sigh for responsible government after the British fashion. Theoretically, I prefer it. But it has scarcely been so successful even in its native habitat that it would be worth a revolution to get it, and it would take almost that to persuade America to adopt a cabinet rather than a Presidential system. I am therefore inclined to think that the best expedient would be a carefully drawn amendment permitting the President to appeal from a recalcitrant Congress to a direct vote of the people. Electrical devices, including the radio, make the distribution of information on the issue easy, and the process of prompt voting relatively simple.

On the other hand, by Constitutional amendment, or perhaps by custom, the President should be required to associate with himself leaders of both houses, from the minority as well as the majority party, and formulate policies and programs which he wishes to lay before Congress, especially in so far as they relate to foreign affairs. The committees of the House and Senate, charged with preparing bills for raising and spending money, should be associated with the President in preparing the budget, and should hold common hearings on all finance bills.

Another grave peril in our Constitutional procedure is the manner of our electing Presidents. Several times it has happened that the man who had the majority in the electoral college, did not even have the plurality of the popular vote. Mr. Roger Babson in his congratulatory message to the President after the 1940 election said that a shift of one per cent of the vote in the right states would have elected his principal opponent.

If that, or anything like that, had occurred, it would have created an exceedingly ugly situation in America, for Mr. Roosevelt would still have had a majority of several millions of the popular vote. So long as Presidential elections are decided by big majorities, nobody is going to worry much about the mathematical fact that, in 1940, one vote in the state of Mississippi had the weight of almost seven votes in New York State or that one vote in Nevada had the weight of more than seven votes in Ohio. But in a close election that disproportion could arouse great wrath.

So long as we keep our two-party system without appreciable challenge from any third party, no one will fear that the vote for a third candidate might be great enough to prevent any candidate from getting a clear majority in the electoral college, and hence throw the election into the House of Representatives, where each state, New York and Nevada alike, has one vote. But even the most devout believer in the advantages of a two-party system will scarcely claim that it is sound democracy or sound policy which thus loads the dice against any third candidate. Unquestionably as recently as 1924 the Constitutional situation cost the elder La Follette, candidate of the Progressive and Socialist Parties, hundreds of thousands, if not millions of votes. I well remember, in campaigning that year, how often I and others heard the Constitutional situation cited as a reason for not voting for La Follette.

Here the Constitutional remedy is clear. The President and Vice President should be elected by a popular vote. Yet I am far from optimistic that an amendment to this effect would be adopted. The less populous states and the states which systematically disfranchise Negroes will find plenty of ways to rationalize their desire to keep their disproportionate power in the Presidential election. It would not, however, take a Constitutional amendment to permit Congress to order that the electoral vote in each state should be divided among the candidates as nearly as possible in proportion to the popular vote. Today, as is well known, the winner takes all, whether he wins by a majority of one, or of one million.

Theorists of government might well raise other questions about the structure of our government. Would it not, for instance, be better that occupational representation should be combined in some way with geographical representation instead of leaving occupational interests to be represented by pressure politics through lobbyists?

What about the unicameral legislature for the nation as well as the states? Why should there be a Vice President? This last question is more pertinent than some may think. Imagine what might have happened to American history if, as a result of accident or illness, Mr. Roosevelt in either of his first two terms had been succeeded by John Nance Garner. Unquestionably it was Mr. Roosevelt and not Mr. Garner who represented the people. It would be a far less dangerous break in continuity if a President, dying in office, should be succeeded either by the head of his own cabinet, presumably in line with his policy, or by the Speaker of the House, representative of the majority party in the more popular legislative body, with perhaps a further proviso that if the unexpired term should exceed a year, the office should be filled by popular vote at the next election.

Of more serious and immediate importance even than these questions, is the inadequacy, under modern conditions, of the forty-eight states for carrying on functions of government which should be decentralized. In no way do state lines conform to natural economic divisions. Almost every great industrial center, grouped around our larger cities like New York, Chicago, Philadelphia, St. Louis and Pittsburgh, contains parts of two or more states. For various of its banking enterprises, the federal government has already set up regions comprising several states. And insofar as decentralization is a matter of geography rather than of functional activity, we shall have to depend more on regions with natural economic boundaries, and less upon states with their arbitrary boundaries unrelated to any natural economic interest. Perhaps this problem can be worked out within the framework of the present Constitution, but it will be difficult.

In spite of these difficulties, I think that, given the present attitude of the Supreme Court, we can make a real beginning on a new social order under the Constitution. At all events, it is premature to dogmatize about the kind of new Constitution we ought to have until we have developed far clearer and more extensive insight into what we want government to do, and how we want government to do it. Today a Constitutional convention would give us a worse rather than a better document. It is healthier now to press for specific amendments than for a convention. That may not be true tomorrow.

In America the weaknesses of our governmental structure and the inadequacies of our social dynamics are both increased by the unsatisfactory condition of our political parties. As we have seen, the Constitution itself by its provisions for the election of the President puts a premium on the two-party system.

There is much to be said for a two-party system. The bewildering multiplicity of parties unquestionably helped to weaken parliamentary government before the fall of the Third Republic in France. It had previously done the same thing in Italy and in Germany.

Nevertheless a two-party monopoly, practically beyond the power of a third party to challenge, is decidedly unwholesome. That is what we have today.

In 1924 Robert M. La Follette, candidate of the Progressives and Socialists, with strong labor backing, got some five million votes. This was a creditable showing, but it fell far short of the expectation of his followers who promptly dropped the effort to form a third party or farmer-labor party. Since 1924 the tendency in America has been more and more toward a two-party monopoly of public interest and even of legal place on the ballot.

There was a period between 1936 and 1938 when it appeared that under the powerful leadership of President Roosevelt, through the primaries and otherwise, the Democratic Party might be made what it had not been—namely a New Deal or Progressive Party as against the more conservative Republican Party. The President's purges, or attempted purges, in 1938, were, however, among the failures of that shrewd politician. They were not consistent, not well thought out, and not well carried through. By 1940, despite the bitterness of class feeling which characterized the campaign,* the programs of the old parties, on the surface, were similar. So were the promises of their leaders in both foreign and domestic affairs. Mr. Willkie was a "yes—but" candidate. The major differences of opinion in American politics are not between the old parties, but those which cut across party lines.

There is a very respectable school of thinkers who accept this fact with satisfaction. They argue that it tends to promote national unity; to checkmate drastic action; to prevent too great bitterness of controversy at the polls. New ideas do prevail, but they must do it by leavening both parties.

One can, of course, make a case along these lines, a case which has certain validity when things are running along smoothly, or, on the other hand, when the chief danger is capricious change. But when one seeks effec-

---

* The showers of vegetables and the like which frequently greeted Mr. Willkie were unprecedented in American Presidential campaigns, and ominous of the spirit that makes an intolerant fascism possible.

tive political machinary for dynamic and constructive change, it is a serious thing that issues are so rarely argued openly, frankly, and constructively in controversies between the major parties.

In four Presidential campaigns, travelling all over America and meeting thousands of people of all classes, I have rarely heard the old party platforms mentioned. People talk about leaders. Not once in my hearing in 1940 did they discuss the old parties. They discussed Roosevelt or Willkie. Most of them voted for—or against —Roosevelt or Willkie. Each leader had a large body of devoted followers to whom he was a Messiah—and that following roughly corresponded to class, and to a less extent nationalistic, lines. But the decisive vote was held by men and women who, quite frankly, decided their choice on the basis of the candidate who they thought was the lesser of two evils. Literally thousands of citizens in all parts of the country—and they must have spoken for tens of thousands or even millions—assured us Socialists that in general they agreed with our position but that they could not throw their votes away. They were afraid that Roosevelt would take us into war quicker than Willkie and so voted for Willkie, or that Willkie would sabotage all the social gains made under the Roosevelt administration. I have hundreds of letters corroborating this statement.

The same thing had happened on a less extensive scale in 1932 before Mr. Roosevelt had proved himself a progressive leader and when both parties were tarred with the same brush of capitalist failure.

Meanwhile, although rank and file citizens discussed not parties but their leaders, the leaders themselves, both Roosevelt and Willkie, felt compelled to compromise with the political machines. Mr. Willkie and his various supporters made a good case against the President because of the prominence of the Hague machine of New Jersey, the Crump machine of Memphis, and, above all, the Kelly-Nash machine of Chicago, in supporting Mr. Roosevelt and especially in "drafting" him at the Chicago Convention. It is certainly true that the President's zeal for reform has not been applied to the municipal machines of his own party, so long as they support him actively. He consented to the "Second Louisiana Purchase" under which Huey Long's successors in Louisiana loyally supported Roosevelt's policy in Washington after income tax proceedings in Washington were dismissed against them.

Attorney General Murphy's solemn promises, some of them made to me, fearlessly to push a thorough investigation of Frank Hague's activities came to nothing. There was an investigation of the situation in Hudson County, New Jersey, by the FBI which, it is understood, went beyond civil liberties questions decided against Mayor Hague by the Supreme Court. It was chiefly my own pressure which was instrumental in getting that investigation. Nothing was heard of the result of it. Mr. Roosevelt may have believed that if he could make the higher righteousness triumph all over the world, he could come back and clean up Jersey City as his subordinates finally helped to clean up New Orleans. At any rate, Mr. Willkie's own relations with the Pennsylvania Republican machine, his own failure to comment on charges pertaining to at least one Republican Mayor which I laid before him, left him in a poor position to criticize his opponent. Under the American scheme of things, political parties are held together far less by principle than by tradition, patronage, and the professional politicians who direct the local machines. Against these cynical and corrupt machines we have made some progress in municipal government; but not too much. Meanwhile not even crusaders seeking the independent vote can neglect the professional operators of their own party machines. Mr. Roosevelt has been very tender of Boss Hague's wishes in most of his judicial appointments in New Jersey.

All these professional operators have heretofore pretty well managed the primaries in the larger cities. That system of reform has not been the source of progress which its founders hoped. It has made it harder, not easier, to get uniform national action on great issues.

American voters do not use primaries on a national, but on a state scale. Each state has its own laws, each state its own problems and its own hopes. There have been occasions when one or another of the old parties has been captured or strongly influenced by progressives through the primaries. But it cannot be said that the primary system has always and everywhere aided the forces of progress and reform. It has, on the contrary, added to the expense of the whole election procedure, and especially in the more populous states made more necessary than ever the functioning of a permanent political machine. Under these conditions the primary system has been one of the many factors which have hindered the growth of a powerful third party or new party in the United States.

In general, despite encouraging exceptions, most of our numerous campaigns, primary and electoral, local, state and even national, are terribly expensive * devices for fooling the people or for preventing that straight thinking which is an inescapable necessity of our political development if we are to avoid confusion and violence. This similarity between the parties, and the popular cynicism with regard to both of them, invite the development of an American type of fascism by making pressure politics at once more necessary for getting things done and more irresponsible. It encourages trust in leaders as men, some of whom may yet resort, with success, to those highly dictatorial anti-democratic practices which Huey Long successfully employed.

Mr. Roosevelt's popularity with the masses has been a real check, thus far, on the emergence of demagogues who can rival the Louisianan's performance. But as I have pointed out, fascism can come to America through the development of existing political institutions and tendencies. It might be in part the result of the work of men who themselves quite honestly hate fascism, or its most offensive features, but cannot or will not understand for themselves, or explain to the people, the dif-

* The 1940 general election, national and local, according to the estimates of the Senate Committee on Elections, cost $45,000,000.

196

ference between true fascism and old fashioned reaction, and who are content with the parties as they are. Hitler himself was no aristocrat or great industrialist, or spokesman for them, but a man of the people and a friend of the "little man" who actually won for his coalition a majority at the polls. An even better example is to be found in the career of Julius Caesar. He belonged to the popular party. He took care of the boys in the Roman political machine out of the proceeds of his conquests. He rejected the crown, and his adopted son and successor, Augustus, who established the empire, did it under the forms of the republic. Something of the sort could happen in America, although I hasten to deny the imputation that Mr. Roosevelt desires to copy Julius Caesar!

These political reflections lead to a problem at least as fundamental as the problems of purpose and plan. I refer to the dynamics of change. Most Americans are convinced, even those who sing the praises of democracy, that its chief danger lies in its tendency to impulsive, ill-considered change. I should be tempted to argue the exact opposite: that the chief danger in a democracy is the inertia of men, their deep-rooted conservatism and traditionalism; their apathy; their willingness to believe that almost any forward-looking program is, as the proverbial expression has it, "too good to be true." In point of fact we men in the mass suffer from both these apparently contradictory tendencies—usually from inertia, but occasionally from willingness to take ill-considered action, especially if that action does not violate our fetishes. Sometimes in a state of high emotional excitement we are ready to destroy in order—we say—to make all things new. Usually, however, special interests, class or regional, are able to exploit inertia and tradition. Witness, for instance, the "rotten borough" system of representation in many of our state legislatures, and the decades of delay in making so comparatively minor and obviously intelligent a reform as the abolition of the "lame duck" sessions of Congress every two years.

There is a homely exhortation against the use of a sledge hammer to kill a cockroach, yet in our social affairs it has taken catastrophe, profound emotional upheaval, war, or violent revolution, to create the conditions under which obviously desirable reforms can be undertaken. Our Civil War and the Reconstruction Period that followed it were about the worst and most costly ways of ending chattel slavery in America. No other ways were found.

But even as I write these words, I remember that in large parts of the world both slavery and serfdom were abolished without war, by happier and quieter processes. I want to emphasize, not reconsider, the case I have already made against the costliness of violent revolution in our complex civilization. Admitting, however, the force of that case; admitting, moreover, that more things have happened in quiet and orderly fashion than we sometimes recall, it still remains true that the problem of stirring up the desire, the will, the imagination to make even comparatively minor changes of importance, and to make them in time, is still to be classed under the head of unfinished business; unfinished business not only for the politician and the educator but for the plain citizen who has suffered so unnecessarily because it has taken disaster to arouse him out of lethargy. Sometimes that disaster has been so overwhelming that it has meant generations of retrogression, not progress, for men.

What's to be done to bring about a more realistic political alignment with more dynamic power? Frankly, I see no clear answer. I am still of the opinion that sound democratic progress by political methods will be immensely furthered by a party which consciously expresses the interest of the workers, both as producers and consumers. I am exceedingly skeptical whether either of the old parties can be captured by adherents of this point of view. On the other hand, for reasons which I have already given in Chapter VI, I no longer think a nationwide labor party in America is practicable or desirable. For many years we Socialists had hoped that, in spite of difficulties, including our Presidential rather than parliamentary system, a party might emerge in America along lines of development, organization, and conviction roughly parallel to the British Labor Party. Today that hope is gone, not to return except perhaps under the stimulus of a remarkable success of the Labor Party in Britain in establishing a new and democratic social order in that country, and in solving the problems of empire.

For the immediate present there is nothing to do but continue our Socialist efforts, reexamine and restate our position in reference to current problems, and build up Socialist Party organization, at least for educational purposes. I do not regret the Socialist campaign of 1940 from this point of view. It is likely that there will be many other campaigns which Socialists will have to enter both to keep alive an idea and to do the foundation work which must be done before any sound structure of a new political party can be built. How that structure will be built is not a subject on which I am today prepared to dogmatize. Any plan would of necessity be profoundly affected not only by America's involvement in war, but by the extent and duration of that war. It will also be affected by the degree of success of international socialism in making new beginnings.

Meanwhile there are certain political tasks to which Socialists have set themselves, and in which they should have the cooperation of believers in democracy who may be skeptical of socialism. I refer especially to the democratization of the process of electing a President. It is essential to democracy to keep open the ballot in forty-eight states to other candidates than those of the major parties. Year by year that task becomes harder. As the law now stands, in such important states as Ohio and California it is virtually impossible for a new party to place itself on the ballot—so many are the signatures required to its petition. In states like Pennsylvania and Michigan the law is more reasonable, but the old parties have taken care to see to it that minor parties or new parties must file election petitions in the early spring, well before the major parties have formulated their platforms or nominated their candidates. The day has passed when men and women profoundly dissatisfied with the Republican and Democratic Conventions can organize a new party as effectively as Theodore Roosevelt organized his Bull Moose in 1912.

To analyze all the tricks by which minor parties are kept off the ballot, and write-in votes are uncounted or rejected, would take disproportionate space in this brief book. Fortunately the American Civil Liberties Union, in cooperation with other interested groups and parties, is setting up a committee to fight further restrictions on the use of the ballot by minority parties, and to win back some of the ground which has been lost. If this effort is successful, I have a very genuine belief that the American public, aroused to what men can do by political action for their own plenty, peace, and freedom, will find a way to express themselves through a new or more adequate political realignment.

We Socialists who expect to keep plugging away at our own organization are willing and anxious to have our organization become the party of tomorrow, but we have no desire to sacrifice our social hopes by insisting that names or organizations dear to us are the absolute essential to the ends we seek.

Keenly as we feel the vicissitudes of the years, we are proud of the generally acknowledged fact that the little Socialist Party pioneered for every major reform the old parties adopted. That has not been enough. We shall go on pioneering for democratic socialization, believing that our work will hasten its coming and inspire the organizations which will bring it.

None of these problems which I have lumped under the head of unfinished business permits easy solution. But given time and freedom from war and the fear of war, more can be done than we may think.

It is that fear which is now before all our eyes as we look at world affairs. I have been trying to write about the America that is, the America that I fear may be, the America that I hope will be. The difficulties which face us as we try to build the bridge to a desirable future for our beloved country are many. They are not, of themselves, insurmountable. It is not primarily our own national problems, economic or political, but the problems of our relation to the war-torn world of which we are a part which threaten to frustrate all our hopes, all our plans for democratic socialization, and to fasten the war system and totalitarianism upon our children and their children—such as may survive—for uncounted generations.

I started out to write this book primarily in terms of our American economic and political problems. From its beginning I could not escape the significance of a second world war in my own generation. To talk about America's future without reference to the world's has been impossible. It is necessary therefore to give special attention to the desperately unfinished business of world organization.

CHAPTER IX ☆ THIS NATION AND WORLD ORGANIZATION

IT WOULD be magnificent if one could say, "my fatherland is the world." Until one can say it in terms of more than idealistic yearning, the quality and permanence of any good society is unsure. The brotherhood of man, regardless of race, creed, color, tribe, or nation long has been the theme of the world's greatest prophets and sages. Today war is again teaching us by its terrors how closely we are tied together, and how impossible it is to expect peace by perpetuating the lines which divide not only men, but nations, into the House of Have and Have Not. Not Mr. H. G. Wells himself believes more fully than I in the value of world organization for world peace.

But what kind of organization; when and how can it be achieved; and by what methods? These questions cannot possibly be answered simply in terms of what ought to be, or what some maker of paper utopias thinks is good. The underlying problems of world union have been ignored or misstated, or the factors involved wrongly estimated, in every plan of which I have knowledge.

On one negative principle we should all agree. No world organization for peace can be successful—it may instead increase the likelihood of war—if, like the League of Nations, it depends primarily on the principle of actual or potential coercion, economic or military, to maintain an uneasy status quo, and to exalt the sanctity of treaties which deny that change and growth which are the law of life. The principle of sound world organization, or any approach to it, must be cooperation in advancing the common well-being.

But how will you get that sort of cooperation? Historically it is true that common interests should find expression in a proper framework of government. Our thirteen original states might easily have become so many warring nations had it not been for the federal principle successfully embodied in our Constitution.

It does not follow, therefore, that the federal principle can suddenly be imposed on the world. It was successful in America precisely because the thirteen colonies did have a common background, and, with the exception of chattel slavery, similar economic conditions. So far was the federal principle as embodied in the Constitution from complete success that the issue of slavery was decided only by the bitter arbitrament of one of the world's great wars. In all history there is no parallel or precedent for imposing organization, federal or otherwise, on a world as deeply divided as the world now is. Historically, religion, geography, language, common economic interest, and military conquest have advanced unification; military force alone has never done the job over any long period of time.

Mr. Clarence Streit's original principle of "Union Now" which he popularized, was a common belief in, and practice of, political democracy. It was a principle which could not possibly sustain the weight which he put upon it. If political democracy had been strong enough to sustain "union now," it would not have collapsed as it collapsed in France. Great Britain and her self-governing dominions have ties of a similar political democracy as well as of common language and tradition, but it is hypocritical nonsense to say that the British Empire is held together by democracy.

It is equally romantic to believe that a democratic form of government of itself possesses the emotional and practical compulsions to unite nations whose economic interests differ sharply.

One of the greatest difficulties, economic and social, is presented by the extent of colonial imperialism. A world order freezing control of the dominant races and nations over most of the earth's surface would be disastrous. No scheme of world organization which I have ever seen gives proper weight to economic factors in general, or to colonial imperialism in particular, or offers reasonable hope of success in dealing with them.

Another factor in our problem which it is blindness to deny is the strength of an emotional nationalism. Never mind how irrational that feeling is, or how comparatively modern its expression, it is enormously strong. Sovereign national states, on the old order, are dead in Europe. That is a fact which time can only confirm. Nevertheless patriotic emotion in many cases will be strengthened, not weakened, by the war. A German reorganization of Europe would probably conform to economic realities more nearly than the old order, but in the conquered countries the idea of liberty will be tied up emotionally and practically with the struggle for complete national independence. It is to be hoped that common hatred of the dominant Nazi bureaucracy will make the peoples of every land think increasingly as Europeans rather than mere nationalists, and act together to achieve a United States of Europe, but the process will probably be slow, and in ardent hearts nationalism (as in Ireland under British rule) will acquire new glory.

In the unlikely event that Germany should be completely defeated, revenge for the past and fear for the future will probably result in another desperate effort to subordinate the German nation to the conquerors. It is expecting a great deal to believe that a triumphant Britain which has achieved empire largely by encouraging through the centuries the disorganization of Europe, will make a disinterested effort to achieve a United States of Europe.

If the war results in some degree of stalemate, we shall probably have to expect the organization of Europe on a new balance-of-power basis between Great Britain and Germany, with Stalin as the unknown quantity. Such a peace would be neither ideal nor permanent. But it is conceivable that the rise of new forces and new methods might transform it into something better without new world war.

We Americans will not be justified in playing a Pharisaic rôle toward Europe because we are about the last people who would, in practice, consent to any great transfer of power to a world government, a union of democracies, or even an English-speaking union (as opposed to an Anglo-American imperial alliance to run the world). Few of our self-styled internationalists, when it came to the point of action, would accept any attainable world or regional state in any near future in which the world government would have power over our government analogous to the power of the government in Washington over our forty-eight states. Yet Mr. Streit and his disciples continually expound this comparison. They defeat their own cause by pressing it to impossible and undesirable lengths.

Certain conclusions are inescapable: First, a desirable world government is an exceedingly unlikely result of this war. Men, women and children are not starved and bombed into sanity. The best we can hope for will be a peace which will make possible a desirable evolution, and the first requisite of such an evolution lies in the field of economic arrangements, rather than political alliances.

Second: No organization of cooperation, economic or political, can be achieved if it rests solely on existing governments and has no roots in the direct loyalty of the constituent peoples to it. In any league or federation the peoples partner to it should be directly represented in its councils—not merely indirectly through the political governments of their own states. International friendships must consciously be built up; and those international affiliations of workers and their organizations which all governments, including our own, now discourage, must be encouraged. Communist dominance of workers' organizations is, of course, a type of red imperialism, the antithesis to democratic affiliation.

So difficult is any plan for complete world organization, that men may be compelled to approach it by beginning with something less than the whole world. Two principles of partial unification are making headway in men's thinking. The first principle would unite peoples on the basis of common language and culture; for example, an alliance of English-speaking people which has become Mr. Streit's immediate concern, or a league of Spanish-speaking peoples, which Spanish fascists desire. The second principle is regional; for example, a United States of Europe which might then be federated loosely with the British Empire, a Pan American federation, and the U.S.S.R.

Both principles present difficulties. An English-speaking union even if it should become a political possibility, is undesirable if it should be conceived in terms of maintaining for a while longer, Anglo-American rule over "the lesser breeds without the law." The American imperialism which, as I have already argued, would mean fascism at home, would not become a blessing by reason of union with Great Britain. Our American prejudices make us singularly unfitted for the rôle of ruler over colored races. Therefore, those of us who look toward any increasing degree of world unity as a basis for justice and peace, should have to oppose an English-speaking alliance as a breeder of war and imperialism, unless and until the aspirations of India were satisfied, and a plan formulated for ending colonial exploitation and imperial monopolization of raw materials.

Our present enthusiasm for British imperialism, as contrasted with Hitler's, must not let us forget that the British Empire was acquired and is maintained by force of arms; that under it the resources of the colored races have been appropriated without even the compensation of a decent educational program for them or an adequate health service. (See on this subject that excellent and generally pro-British book, *Great Britain* by Albert Viton; John Day.)

There is a curious expansion of the idea of the union of English-speaking peoples which has been suggested by certain former Communist fellow travellers. They contemplate hopefully an alliance of Great Britain, the United States, the U.S.S.R., and China which would really be a war alliance against the Axis powers plus Japan. Even though the Roosevelt Administration made a gesture of appeasement to Stalin by dropping the moral embargo on airplanes to his vast territories (and thence to Germany?) the idea is politically unthinkable. Such an alliance could be held together only on the crassest considerations of power politics. (Even in China the Communists and Generalissimo Chiang Kai-shek are, as I write, perilously close to open war.) This project presupposes a non-existent moral distinction between Hitler's and Stalin's totalitarianism, or else it presupposes that Stalin's brand is not dangerous to us. At the moment it is less dangerous, but looking down the years, it is probably even more dangerous to any democratic idealism because it may be more powerful.

On the whole, the most promising beginnings of

federation are probably regional. If it is impossible to build the United States of Europe, considering the unity of European civilization despite her almost constant wars, it will be impossible to build a United States of the World.

Here in the Western Hemisphere, we have made a beginning of some value in Pan Americanism. That beginning has had an artificial quality. Our emotional, cultural and economic relations with Europe, and even with parts of Asia, have been far closer than with large areas of South America. Yet our old tradition, today emphasized by fear of German aggression, unites the Western Hemisphere against interference from the old world. Unfortunately, despite Secretary Hull's good intentions, the attitude of Americans, both in Congress and throughout the country, toward Pan Americanism is flagrantly imperialistic. A South American who had heard the public and private remarks which I have heard all over this country, might have considerable justification for wanting to bargain with Japan or Germany, as a counter-balance to the power of the "Colossus of the North." The strong Aprista Party in Peru and other South American countries, and the Chilean socialists are entirely logical in desiring greater unity or cooperation among South American nations as a prerequisite to a desirable Pan Americanism.* They remember that

* Early in 1941 the old rivals Brazil and Argentina, together with those recent enemies, Paraguay and Bolivia, held a conference on their economic problems and the better joint use of the River Plata. The United States, like Chile and Peru, was represented only by an observer. The conference may mean a beginning of South American regional cooperation on the initiative of the nations concerned.

the United States has once or twice interfered to prevent the growth of such unity in Central America.

So vast is this hemisphere that, even from our own selfish point of view, we ought to recognize that our strongest ties of interest are continental rather than hemispheric. Our military defense is far more bound up with Canada, to the north of us, and the Caribbean regions than with South America below the fringe of the Caribbean. Nevertheless, without forgetting this military fact, I believe in cultivating the maximum possible hemispheric friendship and economic cooperation, which is something different from organic unity or imperial domination. It is a plain fact that a cooperative Western Hemisphere could, if necessary, be completely self-sufficient economically.

So far even this administration has felt compelled to deal with dictators in Latin America, rather than the peoples, to buy their friendship by loans, and to regard any country as at least potentially democratic whose dictator will play ball with us rather than with the Germans. Granting that our government must deal with other governments as they are, neither the Washington Administration nor the American people should forget that real and enduring hemispheric cooperation must depend upon understanding among peoples, and the promotion of a far sounder economy than now exists in Latin America. Our own policy should be to promote that sort of economy, and not to buy up dictators.

Specifically, we should open up our markets to such supplies as we need without the restrictions our high tariff people have forced on us. We ought to encourage diversification of industries in South America and the building up of populations to support them. Under no circumstances should we contemplate the wicked madness of a cartel or any other device to hold back South American products (most of which we can't use) from a desperately needy Europe, but we might make a cartel or other arrangement sufficient to support a South American price level against such barter-bludgeoning as Germany practised against the Balkan States.

Secretary Hull, in his testimony before the House Foreign Affairs Committee, made a true but appalling statement of fact: Said he, "Any country that might get control of the seas in a movement of world conquest, and representing three or four hundred million industrial population, that perhaps lacked 40 per cent of sufficient food, and, further, 60 per cent of raw material for their people to work with, would have every human incentive, being in control of the seas, to lead straight in the direction of the great foodstuffs and raw materials, with none of those countries in a position to defend itself." To which the answer can never be, for any long period of time, mere military force, or the mere elimination of Hitler. It must be a Pan American arrangement which will facilitate decent trade with hungry Europe, not stop it, even if, under present conditions that trade will have to be a kind of glorified barter.

A victorious England would follow about the same trade policy toward South America as a victorious Germany. Even before this war, as Carleton Beals points out in his admirable book, *Pan America*, England had already begun the new streamlined, state-directed trade tactics, which we think of as solely German. England's industrialists and their German colleagues (as Philip La Follette pointedly reminded us in his appearance at the Senate hearings on the Lend-Lease Bill) in February 1939, after Munich, made an agreement at Düsseldorf for trade subsidized by their respective governments, largely directed to the capture of South American trade as against the United States. A post-war Britain will be driven by her debts, her desire to protect her currency, and her imperial policies, to intensify state-directed trade. In 1937 I heard a prominent Englishman in London endorse, half humorously, half seriously, the old saying, "Britain may lose Canada, but not the Argentine."

If our own country will keep its head, cultivate the friendship of its neighbors, and use its economic power to further not only South American but world cooperation, the situation I have pointed out will not be fatal. What is monstrous is the apparent eagerness of certain high-placed Americans to rush, "if necessary," into war in the completely vain hope that a victorious war can revive an economic situation and a type of trade in which at one and the same time we can shut South American products out of our own markets, practise dollar diplomacy when it pleases us, and make the Monroe Doctrine a disguise for our own imperialism. That cannot be done. The alternative is the development of economic cooperation, and a slower development of Pan American political machinery for joint action.

In any intelligent hemispheric agreements Canada cannot be left out. I am not criticizing present arrangements for joint defense when I say that it is an anomalous and potentially dangerous situation when an independent nation (Canada) in alliance with European partners can enter world war in the assurance that she is guaranteed from attack at home by her enemy through the power of a neutral nation (the United States) which she has not in the least consulted.

Unless we should reach arrangements making world war unlikely, or unless the United States should enter an Anglo-American alliance, Canada will have to throw in her lot increasingly with this hemisphere. I think that that will be a natural result of evolutionary forces. It is not something for the United States to insist upon, especially at a time when imperial loyalty is so strong in Canada.

The truth is that all of us are caught in this dilemma: To remove the causes of war requires world organization, economic and political, but so long as we are caught in the war system, we shall have neither the courage nor the imagination to make the necessary changes. That is why any attack upon war requires not merely an effort to remove its causes, but at least an equal effort to substitute methods of resistance to aggression and oppression which do not involve the madness, destruction, and self-frustration of modern war.

There is no more urgent problem for tomorrow's world; it is a problem in our present state of development which lies outside the field of political party platforms, but within the field of religion, education, and cooperative action through labor unions and other organizations which have already learned much about combatting injustice without war.

In the light of the difficulties we have been discussing, a tentative and practical program for the United States might be summarized somewhat as follows:

1. Cultivate Pan American friendship and joint action—but not organic union—between ourselves and the Latin American states carefully refraining from imperial dominance over them. Give special attention to economic cooperation.

2. Abandon all thoughts of the use of armed force to maintain special trade relationships, open doors, or what have you in Asia. To this end, hasten, not delay Philippine independence, make decent trade treaties with the Islands, and ask all the Powers with interests in the Pacific to join us in a treaty pledging ourselves against military intervention in the Islands. Japan might, indeed, break that treaty. She would be less, not more, likely to do so if the islands were no longer our Achilles heel, pawns in a possible game of Far Eastern power politics. Our relations in the whole Far East which should be based on good will and mutual trade interests would be improved if we should end the insult of unilateral Asiatic exclusion, and control immigration by

treaties or the quota system. That would "save face" and yet not give us an insoluble problem of Asiatic migration to these shores.

3. So long as external dangers demand defense, and the nation in overwhelming majority demands that that defense be in the last analysis military, let it be planned as scientifically as may be, taking advantage of our favorable geographic position and the friendship we can cultivate with our neighbors, in terms of defense of our homes and shores against possible attack. Make it clear that we reject the notion of trying to defend "our interests" or "our trade" by military force all around the world; or of intervening to settle European, African, or Asiatic quarrels by force of arms; or even on this hemisphere of playing military overlord down to Tierra del Fuego. The extreme pacifist argument that there is no half-way point between total peace, total trust in other than military power, and readiness for total war has logical force; to find a non-military defense is one of the great requisites in the struggle for peace. But as America now is, there is a chance for a clear, resolute, and effective defense which will not require of us armament economics after the European pattern. That is the enormous blessing our geographic position and economic resources will give us if to them we add a statesmanlike and friendly foreign policy.

4. Recognize that peace whenever it comes depends for permanence upon economic policies including an end of armament economics, equality of access to raw materials, an approach to a world fiscal system and to

uniform labor standards. Economic relations are more fundamental than a political formula.

5. Recognize, also, that since no victor in total war will dictate a peace of this degree of economic cooperation, and since evolution toward it is more likely to take place in a world millions of whose inhabitants have not been made neurotic wrecks by hunger and the terror of total war, the United States should welcome the first reasonable opportunity to mediate in behalf of a negotiated peace. It must be the combatants who negotiate that peace, the English rather than ourselves who must be satisfied that it is at least less evil than war. But it is intellectually as stupid as it is morally unadmirable for us to bid them fight to the last drop of their blood for no more positive formula than the military conquest of Hitler's Germany. Certainly it is a positive duty, as a factor in bringing a decent peace, for us to assure all of Europe that when the guns are stilled, we shall stand ready for practical cooperation in disarmament, and for trade agreements which may bring some assurance of economic security to the "400,000,000 people lacking 40 per cent enough to eat and 60 per cent of enough raw materials."

Beyond these points, I think—but am unwilling to be dogmatic now—that world federation may better come out of specific arrangements concerning common interests between regional federations than from an attempt to federate in world organization the present—or the prewar—welter of nations great and small.

The success of such cooperation must depend upon

more than the relationships among national governments. It will require the understanding loyalty of the peoples and some measure of direct participation by them in the councils of these regional federations, and finally in the government of the world. There can be no lasting or tolerable rule of one dictator over the world or any league of dictators which can endure. We cannot wait for approaches to world cooperation for perfection of the component nations, but we can insist that it is only growth toward world democracy which will make world government a tolerable thing. A healthy federation will depend on common action to get things done—not primarily on agreement to coerce the evildoer. Yet as a world federation gains men's confidence it should be the custodian of the ultimate police power over mankind.

The goal to which we should advance is not a terribly centralized world state, but a great federation of cooperative commonwealths. It is the ultimate revolutionary perspective. Men have dreamed—men still dream—that it may come out of this war if only Hitler can be completely defeated. So it might, but only if there should be a nearly simultaneous revolt of the peoples and the armies against war, a simultaneous demand for bread and peace, freedom and fellowship. Victory will not of itself bring that; neither Hitler's nor Churchill's victory. More and more I am persuaded that this new organization cannot come automatically out of the consuming hates which modern war engenders. The new society will not be built by embittered men in a bankrupt world, even in the fortunate but unlikely event that Ernest Bevin, giving at least lip service to Harold Laski's program, should be prime minister of a triumphant Britain in Churchill's stead.

Three revolutions, Russian, Italian and German, came in the interlude between two world wars. Perhaps in an economic sense they were progressive; in respect to liberty, tolerance, and the dignity of man they were terrifyingly retrogressive. And this because they were born of exhausting war. Hence my interest is in the earliest practicable peace rather than a formula of perfection; in an America which will kindle new hope in the hearts of those now in bondage to dictators by making democracy work; not in an America broken by trying to play God or policeman to a warring world.

If and when at last the guns are stilled, the real struggle will begin. Living and vigorous men, free from the nightmare of this war, may—no, they must—then seek other methods to press toward total democracy, not alone in one nation but in the world. In the realization of this hope lies the future of us all. But in working for it, more than ever should our American formula be: "the maximum possible cooperation for peace; the maximum possible isolation from war."

EPILOGUE

THERE is no record of a nation so richly blessed as ours. Two great oceans are our natural ramparts. They shelter a continent rich in resources on which a people whose origins are in many lands can work out their common destiny, uncursed by the incarnate hates and fears which through the centuries have drenched a troubled Europe in blood. Our history is relatively brief; it has its ugly pages, but it has given us a glorious tradition of liberty. Today we are possessed of all the equipment we need for the conquest of poverty.

But we have not conquered poverty, nor have we succeeded even as well as the peoples of certain other lands in ending unemployment. Our failure, in spite of our advantages, is the failure of a social order whose economic and political loyalties and institutions have nurtured war, poverty, and exploitation, when peace, plenty, and freedom might be ours.

We, to a less degree than Europe, but none the less inescapably, are caught in the revolution which is sweeping away private capitalism and the older types of absolute national states. It is an ugly revolution, confused with a war whose roots spring from national and imperialist rivalries. Into that war we are likely to be drawn by a singular mixture of fear for ourselves, sympathy for the victims of aggression, and mistaken hope that war and preparation for it will give new life to a dying order.

That dying order will not be saved by anybody's military victory. Neither will the defeat of the Nazi power, desirable as that is, guarantee that the new order will be democratic or tolerant. Great Britain is not yet socialist, and British Socialists have not officially proclaimed any policy for the empire or for Europe to which the masses of men outside Britain's borders can rally with even so much confidence as they felt—in vain —in Wilson's Fourteen Points during the First World War. Revolution in Europe might, indeed, follow the military defeat of Hitler, or sheer exhaustion of the combatants, but it would not necessarily be democratic revolution. Stalin's communism, or a variant of it, would have a better chance. Whoever wins will face the urgent and often contradictory hungers of men; for bread, for peace, for security, for power, for freedom. Nobody's victory will assure the Western Hemisphere the right to withhold its resources from the supply of human needs. Nor can it guarantee peaceful permanence to the nations in the House of Have who can find no way of sharing their blessings.

The future of America will be greatly affected by the military result of this war. It will not be determined by it. British or Anglo-American victory in Europe and Asia, if it were possible, could no more restore the old economic and political order than the temporary restoration of Bourbon kings to the throne of France restored feudalism. These facts are usually ignored or forgotten in our absorption in the war.

Under these circumstances we drift with a sense of

fatality rather than of purpose. The drift sweeps us toward our own brand of fascism or totalitarianism which is made our all but certain fate if we are caught in total war.

But this doom need not be ours. Democracy can work; it can utilize our resources and machinery for abundance. It must become "total" in the sense that it must inspire our economic order and arrangements as well as those we now narrowly call political. We have to accept a high degree of collectivism because of the development of the machine age; we can exercise intelligent choice concerning the kind and degree of collectivism and the nature of its control. That is, we can choose democratic socialization or the cooperative commonwealth instead of fascist or communist totalitarianism or chaotic strife.

To the achievement of this good society there is no infallible and dogmatic guide. The process must be experimental and creative. There are principles to inspire us and invaluable lessons to be learned from the records of the recent years, from failure as well as success, even from our tragic disappointments. There are no insuperable logical difficulties in harnessing machinery for life and abundance under a fellowship of free men. We need wisdom and skill in planning. But our greatest need is new hope, new conviction, new loyalties adequate to the task of making our future and our children's bright with the blessings of plenty and peace, freedom and fellowship.

This should be America's task, and through its accomplishment America will most bless mankind. It is a task from which no changing fortunes of a world war —to which we cannot be indifferent—must be allowed to swerve us. Upon our success in this enterprise our future depends, and upon it hangs all our hope of service to mankind.

INDEX

INDEX

A

absentee ownership, 23

acreage, city and country, tax on, 140

After the New Deal, What?, Norman Thomas, 185

age group, shift in dominant, 21

agriculture, 171*ff.*; food-stamp plan in, 175

Agriculture, Dept. of, defense reckoning, 88, 89*ff.*

"Aid to Britain," 69; criticized, 73; extent of, 71, 72; popular fear as basis for movement, 65*fn.*

Alaska, colony experiment in, 22

Alien and Sedition Law, Smith, 80, 82; dangerous features of, 82; intolerance of, 83

Allies, blunders in First World War, 37; early over-confidence, 48; inept diplomacy, 49

Alsop and Kintner, *American White Paper*, 64

Amalgamated Clothing Workers of America, 114

American Colonies, 13

American Federation of Labor, 114, 116*ff.*; estimate of unemployment by, 90

American Labor Party, Communist activity in, 120, 121

American Socialist Movement, sensitivity of, 102; *see also* Socialism

American White Paper, Alsop and Kintner, 64

"Anglo-American Alliance," 207-8, 214

Anti-Semitism, 31

Aprista Party, Peru, 210

appeasement, 53; misconception regarding, 46

armament economics, 1, 14, 27, 55; cost of, 91*ff.*; danger of, 26; its effect on private capitalism, 24; inflation through, 92, 93, 142; as leading to totalitarianism, 92; in 1940 campaign, 68, 69; test of, 88; and unemployment, 90

Austria, 37

Axis powers, anti-democratic, brutal, 31

B

Babson, Roger, 187

Baldwin, Hanson W., 85

Baltic states, 48

Banking and credit, social control necessary, 148-9; speculation, 149

banks, idle money in, 25

Beals, Carleton, *Pan America*, 144, 212-3

Beard and Smith, *The Old Deal and the New*, 20*fn.*

Beard, Charles A., 59, 99

Bebel, August, 40

Berger, Victor, 121

Berle, Adolf A., Jr., *New Directions in the New World*, 148*fn.*

Berlin, 74

Bevin, Ernest, 15, 50-1, 219

Bilbo, Senator, 176

birth control, 165

birth rate, decline of, 22, 165, 173

Blair, John, *Seeds of Destruction*, 19*fn.*, 20*fn.*

blitzkrieg, 49, 62*ff.*

Borden Company, 154

Borsodi, Ralph, 4

hysteria, national, presidential speeches augment, 64ff.

231

Riis, Jacob, 7
Road to War, Walter Millis, 29
Roman Catholic Church, 12
Roman Empire, internal weakness doomed, 9
Roosevelt Administration, 51
Roosevelt, President, 1, 16, 25, 39, 59, 118; Armistice Day speech, 28; at Buenos Aires, 92; at Chautauqua, 56; deal with Japan, 57; influence on London conference, 56; leaning toward British in crises, 58; policies criticized, 73
Roosevelt, Theodore, 4, 7, 8, 201
Royal Air Force, 74, 89
Ruhr, occupation of, the, 37
Russia, 6, 48; degradation of socialism in, 45
Russian Empire, 13, 31
Russian Revolution, 33, 101

S

Salvemini, Professor, 38
Saturday Evening Post, editorial quoted, 147-8
Scandinavia, semi-socialist society in, 15; labor in, 112
Second International of Socialists and Workers, 40; dissolution of, 102
security, not synonymous with democracy, 22
self-determination of nations, 35
selfishness, as impediment to progress, 11
Senate Foreign Relations Committee, 58
Shanghai, 56
Shaw, Bernard, 163
slums, 5, 138; abolition of, 183
Smith, Adam, *Wealth of Nations*, 15
Smith Alien and Sedition Law, *see* Alien and Sedition Law, Smith

Smoot-Hawley Bill, 39
Social Democratic Party, German, 39
social order, old, 1; inadequate loyalties of, 11; *see also* loyalties
social purpose, 27
socialism, after First World War, 101ff.; effect of American alliance on British, 50; post-armistice failure of, 40; present program of, 200
Socialist Party, German, 31
Socialist Platform, on League of Nations, 36; *see also* League of Nations
socialization, relations of war and peace, 53
South America, cooperation with, 211-2; *see also* Hull, Cordell
Spain, 6, 38-9
Stalin, Josef, 30, 42, 53, 123-4; his deal with Hitler, 44; foreign policy record of, 44; war guilt of, 45; union control by, 117
Stalinism, evolution of, 41
state, the absolute national, 12
state capitalism, in Russia and Germany, 43
state intervention, 16
Steffens, Lincoln, 7
Stimson policy, of non-recognition in Far East, 56
Streit, Clarence, 204, 207-8
Stresemann, Gustav, 36-7
strikes, 7; unsocial danger in, 159-60
Structure of the American Economy, National Resources Committee, 19fn.
subsistence goods, markets for, 21
Supreme Court, profound change in, 185; Witnesses for Jehovah case, 80-1
Sweden, 158

working class, communist theory of international, 42

world organization, dilemma regarding, 214; economic factors, 205; effect of emotional nationalism on, 205; outlook for federation, 217-8; principles of, 203ff.; program for U. S., 215ff.

World Population, Carr-Saunders, 80

World War, First, 4, 6, 8, 12, 13, 19, 47; causes of, 29; imperialist character of, 28-9; lost opportunity in, 33

World War, Second, 8, 15; American relations to, 60, 70, 71; basic origins of, 46; democracy and culture at stake, 32; imperialist in origin, 30

Y

Yangtse River, 57